MARTHA SIMM
1624-166

The front cover *illustration is from an etching by Robert Spence, courtesy of Friends House Library, London. It depicts Martha Simmons and other religious enthusiasts accompanying James Nayler, in October 1656, on his ill-fated entry into Bristol.*

The back cover *facsimile is also courtesy of Friends House Library, London.*

2009 © Bernadette Smith M.Phil

ISBN 978-1-85072-389-9

This book is based on a thesis by Bernadette Smith which she submitted in 2001 to the University of Birmingham for her degree of Master of Philosophy.

Details of Bernadette Smith's thesis can be accessed at www.library.bham.ac.uk./ giving 24 hours notice to see the thesis (on library site only) or contact: The Library, University of Birmingham, Edgbaston, Birmingham B15 2TT. Tel. 0121 414 3344.

Printed in 11 on 12 point Plantin
by Sessions of York
The Ebor Press
York, England

TABLE OF CONTENTS

ACKNOWLEDGMENTS

To Dr Maureen Bell of Birmingham University for supervising the thesis in which this book originated.

Somerset Archive and Record Service for assistance with County and Diocesan Records relating to Martha Simmon[d]s.

Library, Friends House, London.

Library, Woodbrooke Quaker Study Centre, Birmingham.

Rev. Graham Witts, Vicar of Meare, Somerset for his assistance with the history of Meare.

To my husband, Rev. John MacDonald Smith for his assistance with theological matters and for his love and support.

INTRODUCTION

ONE OF the most interesting and significant developments in the history of women's writings was the dramatic increase in publications by women during the Civil War and Interregnum. Prior to 1640 it was unusual for a woman to appear in print and one who chose to follow such a course usually prefaced her work with a justification for participating in an activity considered to be a male prerogative. As late as 1695 Anne Finch, Countess of Winchilsea, would say:

> Alas! A woman that attempts the pen
> Such an intruder on the rights of men.[1]

The English Civil War was one of a number of complex, but related factors which enabled women to engage in the public arena of political and religious controversy. Firstly, on a practical level, as in all wars, women were obliged to undertake tasks traditionally carried out by men, thus acquiring new skills and a degree of empowerment. But the events connected with the war – the religious, social and psychological impact of the Regicide, the establishment of Parliamentary government, the collapse in state censorship and the consequent deregulation of the press – had a much greater significance than the war itself.

In many ways the Civil War was a pivotal moment in the development of women's publications. As Patricia Crawford's evidence demonstrates, between 1616 and 1620 only eight publications were by women but in the half decade 1646-1650 the number had risen to sixty-nine.[2] The largest single group of women to appear in print were Quakers who published more than half of the surviving texts published between 1650-1660. This figure does not reflect the number of Quakers in society as a whole, and furthermore, it does not necessarily reflect the proportion of women's texts which were published and no longer survive. The press played an important part in Quaker life and mission and all their texts have been preserved.[3] Nevertheless, these statistics indicate not only the level of literacy among Quaker women, but also that they were able to take the dangerous step of making their voices public, through preaching, producing pamphlets and broadsides and engaging in the public struggle for religious freedom at a time when a woman was morally if not legally censured for such behaviour.

Appearing publicly in print was one of a number of ways in which women crossed the boundaries between the private and the public; in his *Journal* George Fox encouraged the Friends to proclaim the gospel 'by word, by writing and by signs'[4] and Martha Simmons was one of the earliest Quakers to express her faith in these three ways. She was active in the Quaker movement from her conversion in 1654, when the Quaker mission spread from the north of England to London, until her death in 1665. Around 1655 she became acquainted with James Nayler, a contemporary of George Fox and a leading Quaker. Nayler evidently was an extremely charismatic preacher and leader who gathered around himself a small group of followers, both men and women who were drawn to what they saw as a Christ-like figure. By 1655, some of this group were beginning to vocalise a preference for Nayler over Fox and urged him to challenge the leadership. Martha Simmons, her husband and a small group of other Quakers formed the core of this group and in October 1656, they accompanied Nayler in what was judged to be a dramatic re-enactment, or 'sign' of Christ's entry into Jerusalem. The party were arrested and Nayler suffered horrendous physical punishment and imprisonment for which some historians and literary critics have held Martha Simmons responsible. In spite of the fact that she was not alone in this event, she was indeed a participant. Nayler himself seems to have established this interpretation of events according to his colleague, George Whitehead, who described his downfall as satanically motivated and believed that:

> He [Nayler] came to be ensnared through the subtle Adversary's getting advantage upon him by means of some persons who too much gloried in him ... so it came to pass, according as J.N. related to me, ... that a few forward, conceited, imaginary women, especially one Martha Simmonds, grew somewhat turbulent ... that he came to be

clouded in his judgement ... The substance of the forego-
ing relation, how J.N. came to be ensnared and to such a
loss, he himself gave me the account.[5]

Thomas Simmonds[6] wrote to his wife Martha while she was in
Bristol jail and accused her of being the ringleader of the event:
'surely thou wast the chief leader in that action.'[7] This was used as
evidence against Martha during her examination:

This Martha Simmons is a considerable person. For her
Husband (who tis like knoweth her) tells her, *for she was the
leader* in this action, and gives them a handsome frump for
their foolery to do that work.[8]

Martha could well have instigated the event, for a reading of her
texts indicates that the *adventus* of Christ into Jerusalem, and its
eschatological[9] meaning, represented something to her which was
deeply connected with her own personal conversion. This has to
be balanced by Nayler's deeply christological identification[10] and
the most accurate answer to who among the party was the origi-
nator is that none of them was individually responsible.

The two earliest modern biographers of Nayler; Mabel
Brailsford and E. Fougelklou, describe Martha Simmons as 'the
villain of this piece' coming into Nayler's life 'like a whirlwind ...
to cause havoc.'[11] Nayler's recent biographer, Leo Damrosch in
1998 is more sympathetic and concedes that she 'was clearly not
the madwoman Quaker writers chose to depict her as being.'[12]
Among literary critics as well as biographers, Martha Simmons has
been read only in relation to Nayler's story and consequently her
own texts have rarely been considered worthy of mention in their
own right. Perhaps the most derogatory critic is Andrew W. Brink
who, following the argument of Whitehead, argues that Milton saw
in Martha Simmons the model for Eve and compares Eve's
supposed deception of Adam to Simmons' part in Nayler's downfall. Brink continues to argue that Simmons:

would not leave him [Nayler] alone in London or in Bristol,
following him ... much as Satan tracked Eve until he [Satan]
implanted the self-destructive idea of becoming a goddess.[13]

He refers to her as a 'possible witch,' a 'Ranterish woman,'
(although in a footnote remarks that the records of seventeenth
century witchcraft make no reference to a Martha Simmons).
According to Greaves and Zaller she, 'engineered Nayler's so called

messianic entry into Bristol'[14] and Margaret Drabble also mentions her only as an adjunct to Nayler and makes no mention of her own writings.[15] Kenneth Carroll, while attempting to render a sympathetic account of the Simmons and Nayler relationship, approaches the Bristol event entirely from Nayler's viewpoint and uses language which precludes any discussion of Simmons as a political agent but stereotypes her into the same role of dangerous woman, and casts Nayler in the role of victim:

> Not even in Bristol was the ailing Nayler safe from Martha Simmonds, for she followed him there in order to bring him under her control.[16]

In effect, he totally depoliticises her as does the title of his essay, which refers to her as an 'enigma.' Most recently, Douglas Gwyn has given a more sympathetic reading of her texts, but again, only in reference to Nayler and to what has become known among historians as 'the Bristol event.' Martha Simmons was undoubtedly influential in Nayler's ministry, as he was in hers, but if we look more closely at her life we see that her relationship with him was brief and a critical reading of her texts, letters and transcripts of her spoken words reveals an articulate and engaging woman with courage and energy.

In the last decade sympathetic accounts of Martha Simmons' activities have begun to emerge with the work of Rosemary Moore and Phyllis Mack.[17] The Quaker theologian, Christine Trevett, offers an alternative and refreshingly sympathetic account of Martha Simmons, rightly observing that Nayler's male followers were equally active in the event and the correspondence found on James Nayler revealed that not only the women, but both Thomas Simmonds and John Stranger, husbands of the female protagonists, addressed Nayler in christological language.[18] The American feminist theologian, Rosemary Radford Reuter, is also sympathetic to the women in Nayler's history, but she and Trevett stand alone in their assessment of the female followers of James Nayler and even they offer no analysis of her writings.[19]

Reuther's thesis identifies two distinct categories of feminist writers in the mid seventeenth-century: the 'humanists' and the 'prophets.' Humanists, she argues, are those with access to a classical education, 'usually Anglicans' who did not question the status quo of English religious tradition, while the latter group are so called because of their dissenting religious views and their apocalyptic language.[20] This group of women is today among those whom Sheila Robotham described as 'hidden from history,' and 'hidden from plain sight.'[21] Martha Simmons has been among this hidden group of women for four centuries and I hope to address that imbalance.

The primary sources in this research are Martha's printed texts: *When the Lord Jesus entered Jerusalem* (1656), *A Lamentation for the Lost Sheep of the House of Israel* (1656), and *O England, thy Time is come* (c.1657-8), a later pamphlet, which she co-authored with Hannah Stranger, William Tomlinson and James Nayler. Two other pieces of textual evidence are her signature to the 1659 Quaker Women's Petition[22] and a letter to William Dewsbury. The petition was a document signed by approximately seven thousand Quaker women and presented to Parliament to plead their objection to the payment of tithes. It was printed at the 'Black Spread Eagle,' the home and workshop of Giles and Elizabeth Calvert with whom Martha Simmons probably lived before her marriage in 1655. Secondly, I have also examined the evidence of documents relating to her activities from early Quaker records and correspondence, and thirdly, I have considered her reported speech in transcripts of her examination as it was reproduced in one of my primary sources of evidence, *A True Narrative of The Late Examination, Tryall and Sufferings of James Nayler*, 1657[23] including what she was quoted as saying third hand e.g. her words as reported in a letter from Hubberthorne to Margaret Fell.

NOTES

1. Anne Finch, *The Poems of Anne Finch, Countess of Winchilsea*, (1695) ed. Myra Reynolds, Chicago, 1903, p.4. Quoted in Patricia Crawford, 'Women's Published Writings 1600-1700', in Mary Prior, (ed.) *Women in English Society*, London, 1985, p.227.

2. *ibid*, pp.211-282.

3. Friend's House Library, London has copies of all surviving Quaker texts from the seventeenth century to the present day. Unfortunately, many are only able to be read on microfilm, due to their fragile condition.

4. Norman Pennington (ed.) *Journal of George Fox*, Cambridge: Cambridge University Press, 1911, vol. 1, p.407.

5. George Whitehead, *A Collection of Sundry Books, Epistles and Papers, Written by James Nayler, Some of which were never before Printed, With an Impartial Relation of the Most Remarkable Transaction Relating to his Life*, London, 1716, pp.6-7, quoted in full in Leo Damrosch, *The Sorrows of the Quaker Jesus*, New York: Harvard University Press, 1996, p.118.

6. The name of Thomas Simmonds is spelt variously as 'Symonds,' 'Simmonds' and 'Symons,' but as the most frequently occurring is 'Simmonds' this form has been used throughout this thesis, for husband Thomas; whereas, in the hope of clarification between husband and wife, references here are mostly to Martha Simmons, as on her 1655 Title Page (reproduced on back cover) even though elsewhere the contemporary imprint is Martha Simmonds!

7. Thomas Simmonds to Martha Simmons, 1st November, 1656, reprinted in Robert Rich and William Tomlinson, *A True Narrative of the late Examination, Tryall and Sufferings of James Nayler*, London, 1657, pp.20, 21.

8. *A True Narrative*, p.22.

9. Doctrine of death, judgement, heaven and hell.

10. See Carole Spencer, 'James Nayler: Antinomian or Perfectionist?' in *Quaker Studies*, 6, (1) 2001, pp.106-117.

11. Mabel Richmond Brailsford, *A Quaker from Cromwell's Army: James Nayler*, London: the Swarthmore Press, 1927, p.98. E. Fougelklou, *James Nayler, the Rebel Saint*, London: E. Benn, 1931, p.161.

12. Leo Damrosch, *The Sorrows of the Quaker Jesus*, London, 1996, p.146.

13. Andrew W. Brink, 'Paradise Lost and James Nayler's Fall', *Journal of the Friends Historical Society*, 53, (1), 1972, p.106.

14. Greaves, Richard L. and Zaller, Robert, *A Biographical Dictionary of British Radicals in the Seventeenth Century*, Brighton: Harvester, 1984, vol. 3, p.175.

15. Margaret Drabble, *The Oxford Companion to English Literature*, Oxford: Oxford University Press, 2000, p.714.

16. Kenneth Carroll, 'Martha Simmonds, A Quaker Enigma', *Journal of the Friends Historical Society*, 53, (1), 1972, pp.31-52.

17. Rosemary Moore, *The Light in their consciences*, Pennsylvania: Pendle Hill, 2000. Phyllis Mack, *Visionary Women*, California: University of California Press, 1992.

18. Christine Trevett, 'The Women around James Nayler, Quaker: A Matter of Emphasis' *Religion*, 20, 1990, pp.249-273.

19. Mary Garman et al., *Hidden in Plain Sight*, Pennsylvania: Pendle Hill, 1996, introduction by Rosemary Radford Reuther, p.6.

20. Rosemary Radford Reuther, 'Prophets and Humanists: Types of Religious Feminism in Stuart England,' *Journal of Religion*, 70, 1990, pp.1-18.

21. Sheila Rowbotham, *Hidden from History: 300 Years of Women's Oppression and the Fight Against It*, London: Pluto Press, 1973.
22. *These several Papers Was sent to the Parliament the twentieth day of the fifth Moneth, 1659 Being above seven thousand of the Names of the Hand-maids and Daughters of the Lord*, London, 1659.
23. Richard Rich and William Tomlinson, 1657. Tomlinson was a supporter of Nayler and co-authored *O England* with Nayler and Martha Simmons.

Church of St Mary and All Saints, Meare,
near Glastonbury, Somerset.

Entry in Parish Register for Mary Calvert's burial in 1607.

Entry in Parish Register for the first Martha Calvert's baptism
in September 1607.

Entry in Parish Register for Jane Calvert's burial in 1630.

Chapter One

THE LIFE OF MARTHA SIMMONS

... before ever I saw the Light of the Sun, or received a
natural birth in this visible World, I was rejected of men,
for my Parents denied me a birth; and as concerning self,
it had been good I had not been born; for I have not had
pleasure in this world, but have stood as one alone ...
(*Oh My Beloved*, 1.24)

Childhood and Early Life

The name of Martha Simmons would have been well known among the members of the London book trade in the 1650s as her husband, Thomas Simmonds, and her brother Giles Calvert, were the first two major Quaker publishers. Little is known however of her early life and the sources of information from which it might be constructed are scant and not always reliable. It is possible in spite of this dearth of factual evidence to conjecture with a certain degree of confidence the most likely course of her life from her writings, which form her spiritual autobiography. We also have the evidence of early Quaker correspondence[1] and documentary evidence from other archives.

The Parish records for Meare, the small village in the peat area of Somerset three miles from Glastonbury, where Martha Simmons was born and spent her early years, tell us that she was baptised in St Mary's Church, in the parish of Meare, on the 18th January 1623/4.[2] Her father, George Calvert, was then the Vicar and as the Baptismal Rite of the English Prayer Book stipulated Baptism to be on the eighth day it is reasonable to assume this would have been duly performed making Martha's date of birth 10th January. She was the youngest child of Calvert's second marriage to Ann Collier. His first marriage to Mary Calvert had borne five children of whom only one, Sampson, the eldest child, survived to adulthood and followed his father's path to Cambridge and the priesthood. Of the three later children, Robert died at the age of eighteen and was buried in Meare on 28th January 1618; his brother George was buried just two months later, on 3rd March.[3] Mary died in 1607 at the age of five, while the youngest child, Martha died in 1622 at the age of fifteen, hardly more than a year before the birth of the second Martha Calvert. George Calvert's wife, Mary died in 1607, possibly in childbirth or shortly after the birth of Martha who was not baptised until September 1607. Mary was buried in Meare on the 17th January 1607.[4] In the following year George Calvert married Ann Collier in her home parish of Backwell, on 4th February 1608/9 by licence, the bondsmen being Thomas Mydlam of Wookey, clerk, and John Fisher junior of Meare, yeoman.[5] George and Ann Calvert had seven children of whom four, Elizabeth, Giles, George[6] and a second Martha, survived to adulthood.

Life in the Calvert household can only be pieced together by conjecture and the few sources of information available describe a far from happy situation. From the onset of his ministry and throughout its early years George Calvert seems to have been a difficult man although a rather colourful character. He fell from favour with his congregation early in his incumbency and various complaints were registered against him not the least of which was for drunkenness. He made at least four appearances before the Bishop's court at Wells. Calvert occupied the incumbency of Meare on 27th March 1601 and just one year later, on the 12th July 1602 appeared before the Ecclesiastical Court charged with refusal to observe the form of worship presented in the Book of Common Prayer. This was the first of at least three further appearances before the court, in March and September 1602 and again in December 1603. One of the more bizarre of his misdemeanours and one which proved a cause for complaint was at a baptism service when he refused to hold the child in his arms and ordered one of the god-parents out of the church for refusing to hold the child while he (Calvert) performed the baptism rite. Eventually he called his wife to the church in order to hold the baby for him. Other complaints were that he preached for too long or not at all. Another time he allegedly began the service so early that it was over when his congregation arrived. The most significant charge against him was his refusal to conduct services in accordance with the Prayer Book,[7] which tells us he held puritan views. After his marriage to Ann in 1608 his behaviour seems to have settled down and he remained Vicar of Meare for a further twenty years without comment until his death in 1628. George Calvert was buried in the churchyard of Meare on 16th August 1628.

Financially, life would have been difficult with a family of young children as the stipend for a parish priest in 1601-1627 would not have exceeded £20 per annum and Meare was not a wealthy incumbency. Calvert's death, in August 1628, left Ann with five children. Shortly before his death, their eldest child, Giles, had been apprenticed on 30th June, to the London bookseller, William Luggar.[8] Apprenticeship records of the Stationers' Company state that the indenture was broken shortly afterwards and it is possible he returned to Meare for a while because of his father's death.[9] Another son George, was also apprenticed to the London book trade in 1637 and three daughters remained: Elizabeth, born in 1610 and possibly living away from Meare,[10] Jane, born in 1622 and Martha, the youngest child aged three. Ann Calvert probably remained in Meare for at least two more years until Jane Calvert died in 1630 and was buried in the churchyard of Meare on 17th August, 1630. There is no record of Ann's burial and she presumably left Meare around this time or shortly afterwards.[11]

The Education of a Quaker

Social status and financial resources were the main factors in determining the education of all women in the early seventeenth century and as the daughter of a clergyman on a stipend of no more than £20 per annum, Martha Calvert would have had nothing other than a very basic education. There is no record of a school in Meare in the seventeenth century, so Ann Calvert would probably have taught her children to read and write. Vicars were generally not well off and had an unreliable income. Following the dissolution of the monasteries, the Elizabethan bishops delegated the care of the laity to smaller areas under the care of a rector whose collective rights were known as the 'rectory.' A 'tithe' (Anglo Saxon for tenth) was essentially a tax of one tenth of a man's income paid in kind e.g. every tenth sheaf of wheat. If the rector were unable or unwilling to serve the parish himself he would appoint a legal substitute, the Vicar (Latin Vicarius or Vice). The rector's duty was officially to pay the Vicar a part of his receipt of tithes but in practice this was not always strictly adhered to. Rectors therefore were generally much wealthier than vicars and in many parishes there would have been both: once appointed neither could be removed from his position. The village of Meare was only three miles from Glastonbury, which had been a place of pilgrimage throughout the Middle Ages and was still a centre of religious activity but had been impoverished, like so many other towns, by the dissolution of the monasteries.[12] George Calvert's share of the tithes would have been small. The payment of tithes would later become one of the greatest controversies between the Quakers and Parliament and was an issue to which Martha makes explicit reference in all her texts and active objection in signing the Petition of 1659. What George Calvert said to his household regarding his receipt of tithes can only be surmised but he could not have had any personal influence on Martha's educational and spiritual development, as she was only three years old on his death. Indirectly however his influence may well have been considerable.

Martha Calvert was the child of educated parents and younger sister of an educated man, Sampson, the eldest child of the family and son of Calvert's first marriage to Mary. Like his father, Sampson attended Cambridge and was ordained to the priesthood. We can assume that there would have been a considerable number of books in that home and without a doubt, the King James (Authorised) version of the Bible with which they would have been familiar. The church of Meare also contained stained glass with images of Biblical scenes, principally the Lord's Supper, and the Baptism of the Lord, which had not been removed at the Reformation unlike those in most churches. It is possible that 'an ancient painting, on the top of which is the Cross triumphant in the clouds, surrounded by the celestial choir' was in the church during George Calvert's incumbency but we unfortunately do not know. If these images were in the church in Martha's lifetime the image of the Crucifixion would have been firmly implanted.[13] It is possible that Calvert's first wife and the mother of Sampson, had means to sponsor her son's education or had relatives who would have helped, but Ann Collier does not appear to have had independent financial means and if the son's education is a reflection of the household finances of the family, the Calverts were in more straightened circumstances during the latter years of George Calvert's life. There is no documentary evidence of his wife's activities after his death but it is almost certain that she remained in Meare until 1636 when Jane Calvert died. During the reign of James I there were special charities established to assist the widow of a clergyman in providing herself with a livelihood and it is possible she was a beneficiary of these but there is no evidence.

The London Years

Giles Calvert was freed from, i.e. completed his apprenticeship in 1639 and possibly, around this time Martha and her mother moved to London, where Sampson, by now a priest, was also established. Martha, by now aged thirteen or fourteen, most probably lived with Giles, whose premises were at the Black-Spread Eagle in St Paul's. In *A Lamentation for the Lost Sheep of the House of Israel* she describes how after several years of living in London she began a period of seven years of searching among the various religious sects for a faith, which would satisfy her spiritual quest:

> ... having had a habitation in the City of London sometime; for seven years to-gether I wandered up and down ... and then for about seven years more he kept me still from running after men, and all this time I durst not meddle with any thing of God.[14]

The two seven year periods could be the actual number of years but a biblical appropriation of the number seven is more likely.[15] Martha's years in London were probably the most formative in terms of the influence of literary and religious texts and their writers. She would later in life be referred to as the 'sister to that seller of irreligious book titles Giles Calvert'[16] and clearly Giles was the one with whom she was most associated. He was not only one of the most prolific publishers but published a uniquely wide range of material including many books by the continental mystical writers who shaped the emergence of Quakerism.[17] The earliest of these were works by Saltmarsh (1645), Winstanley (1646) and Richard Farnworth (1647). One third of Calvert's entire output during the decade 1640-1650 was by Quaker writers. He published three texts by James Nayler in 1653 and by 1655 fifty percent of Calvert's publications were those of Quaker writers including Martha's first publication, *A Lamentation for the Lost Sheep of the Home of Israel.* Calvert was one of the more significant publishers of European mystical writers[18] whose spirituality would later be absorbed into the developing radical political climate of England, which culminated with the emergence of the developing Quaker and millenarian spirituality.[19] In 1647 Calvert published Mary Gary's *A Word in Season to the Kingdom of Heaven* and Elizabeth Avery's *Scripture Prophecies Opened.* In the following year, Gary's *The Resurrection of the Witnesses* appeared with two further publications in 1651. These were the only females to appear in Calvert's publications up to this point and may have influenced Martha considerably if for this fact alone. No further women appear in print in Calvert's lists until 1655 with works by Anne Audland and in 1656, Anne Gargill's *A Warning to the World* was published. Although women were never more than a minute percentage of his authors, the trend was upward and the number of Quakers increasingly significant

Words, Writing and Signs

The years of the Civil War and Interregnum were marked by military conflict and religious debate surrounding episcopacy, Presbyterianism and the legitimacy of the Church of England dominated Martha's early adult life, for her writings reveal her quest for a religion, which would satisfy her longing for lasting peace. She seems to have spent time going from one place of worship to another.

In July 1654 the Quakers extended their missionary campaign; George Fox later wrote that they went:

> to spread themselves in the service of the gospel, to the Eastern, Southern and Western parts of the nation: as Francis Howgill and Edward Burrough to London.[20]

Isabel Butler, accompanied by a few other women arrived with a large supply of Quaker tracts, which were sold on Sundays in the yard of St Paul's Cathedral.[21] Until this time the Quaker meetings had been held in the Friends' homes but as the number of conversions increased it became necessary to have a regular meeting place. In March 1655 they secured a large mansion house, which adjoined Aldersgate:

> Some part of an Ancient Great House or Building within Aldersgate was taken for a Meeting place the other part of

it with a Yard being before made a Public for Carriers and Travellers which having for a sign the Bull and Mouth occasioned the meeting to be held there to be known and distinguished by the Name of Bull and Mouth or Bull Meeting which was the first Publick Meeting Place taken and set apart for that service where Meetings were held ... and so continued until the dreadful burning of the City when the same was laid in Ashes.[22]

Thomas Simmonds,[23] who had previously been a Birmingham bookbinder, moved to London in 1655.[24] The earliest evidence for a connection between Thomas Simmonds and the Calverts is the imprint of the 1652 publication by Thomas Hall, *The Font Guarded with XX Arguments:*

> *London, Printed by R. W. for Thomas Simmons, Book-seller at the sign of the Bible in Birmingham in Warwickshire* and to be sold in London by *George Calvert* at the sign of the half Moon in *Paul's* Church-Yard 1652.

Thomas Simmonds is variously referred to as a bookbinder, bookseller and printer but the difference was rather fluid and it is impossible to say what his original trade was. He married Martha Calvert in 1655 (when she was 31) and was established as a bookseller by 1656, at The Bull and Mouth, with the help of Giles Calvert. The Bull and Mouth became a focus of Quaker activity and one of the main outlets for Quaker publications. It remained so until destroyed by the Great Fire of 1666.

James Nayler, one of the leading Quaker figures, was born at Ardsley Hall, West Yorkshire, in 1617[25] into a farming family and volunteered for service with the Parliamentary forces in 1642, eventually becoming a Quartermaster under General John Lambert. He met George Fox in 1651 at the home of Fox's neighbour, Lieutenant Roper, and was profoundly influenced by Fox's preaching. Nayler joined the Quaker campaign and in 1652 travelled with Fox and Richard Hubberthorne to Swarthmoor Hall, the home of Judge Thomas and Margaret Fell. He was a charismatic figure who became influential in the Quaker movement during the London mission of 1654 when he joined Francis Howgill and Edward Burrough. He arrived in London in 1654 and where George Fox's influence had failed Nayler's was particularly successful. The difference seems to have been in his style of preaching which one convert described as 'words exceedingly serviceable to me like arrows to my heart.'[26] His popularity was such that divisions in loyalty soon developed which were compared to the divisions of the Church in Corinth[27] but according to Edward Thomas,[28] the particular intimacy between him and his followers did not begin until Edward Burroughs returned to London from his visit to Bristol in the spring of 1656. It is impossible to say for certain how Martha met Nayler but we know from correspondence between Alexander Parker and Margaret Fell that he visited Giles Calvert's house:

> Afterwards Ja[mes] N[ayler] and I passed down to Giles Calverts and we found him (Calvert) there.[29]

Simmons' relationship with Nayler is not documented directly by either of them and therefore we can only deduce their tie from the evidence left by others and from the numerous elliptical references to him in Martha's texts. Shortly after her conversion Martha seems to have been gripped by zeal for spiritual truth and began travelling and preaching, interrupting meetings. In *O England* Martha refers to her visit to Colchester where she was imprisoned on more than one occasion. One of these was in December 1655, possibly to visit Parnell, who later wrote to William Dewsbury that:

> Our tender sister, Martha Simmondes is here in Bondes in the Towne prison; she was put in the last evening for speakeing to a priest; she hath beene in twice before this within a weeke but they had not power to keep her ...[30]

Martha had become very active in the Quaker movement by 1655 and around the Calverts and Simmons a coterie of radicals grew up. Among these were Hannah Stranger and her husband John, a combmaker, and we can reasonably assume that some of the other radical Quakers whose works were published by Giles Calvert such as Anne Gargill were familiar people in both households. Along with two other Quaker women, Hannah Stranger and Dorcas Erbury, she began travelling around London and further afield, interrupting meetings and questioning vociferously the authority of the leading Quaker leaders in openly confrontational behaviour: she would later say of this period of her life that she was 'moved to declare to the world'[31] and that she was often misjudged. She travelled around the south of England proclaiming her faith in word and signs: on one occasion she went partially naked with sackcloth and ashes on her head as a sign. The dominant male leaders,

16

Francis Howgill and Edward Burroughs were unsympathetic to Martha who turned to James Nayler for support. Martha herself during questioning by magistrates in Bristol gave the account of what actually took place:

> Being among the people called *Quakers* in London, I was moved to declare to the world, and often they would judge me exceedingly, that I was too forward to run before I was sent and that nevertheless I loved them well, as being men of pure life but I was moved by the power, I could not stay though they sometimes denied me, yet I was forced to go and my word did prosper, and the last service I was in was Ware and Hartford, and there I was faithful and then I came to London to them and then we were all one, and when I came I did not know what I should do further and then I was moved of the Lord to go to James Nailer, and tell him I wanted Justice, and he being harsh to me, at length these words came to me to speak to him, which I did and struck him down; How are the mighty men fallen, I came to Jerusalem and behold a cry, and behold and oppression, which pierced him and struck him down with tears from that day and he lay from that day in exceeding sorrow for about three days, and all that while the power arose in me, which I did not expect seeing I knew he was in that condition: But after three daies he came to me and confessed. I had been clear in service to the Lord.[32]

Her evidence suggests she spent most of the summer of 1656 travelling and preaching throughout the South of England and as we know she had contacts in Bristol, through parts of her home county of Somerset. Impelled by apocalyptic expectations she began to demonstrate public signs or dramatic re-enactments of liturgical events. On another occasion while preaching in Colchester, according to Parnell she was 'moved to walk in sackcloth barefoot with her hair spread and ashes upon her head.'[33] Occasionally other Quaker men and women were given to individual public demonstration by walking barefoot, sometimes dressed in sackcloth and occasionally partially, or even wholly, naked as a sign of innocence.

The summer months of 1656 saw the development of an apocalyptic movement among a small group of Quaker women of whom Martha was the leader. Their belief in the imminent coming of

Christ 'this very year'[34] prompted some enactment of signs and preaching. Martha was reproached for what was seen as obtuse behaviour by the existing Quaker leaders whereupon she sought support from Nayler but he failed to meet her request and in her words, was 'harsh' to her. Later he seems to have had a change of heart and according to Martha admitted that he had wronged her. What Martha says of her own change of heart during the three days Nayler spent with her is significant: 'the power arose in me.' But what follows is of even greater significance in the development of events between 1655 and 1657, for she says of Nayler: 'And then he lay at my house three daies.' The similarity between the three days of Christ in the tomb followed by the Resurrection and the three days during which both Martha and Nayler undergo a period of spiritual re-discovery and empowerment would not have been unnoticed by contemporary readers. What actually took place is difficult to ascertain as accounts differ. Half a century after the events, George Whitehead wrote:

> For so it came to pass according as J.N. related to me some time after the Lord had restored him out of his bewildered and suffering state, that a few forward, conceited, imaginary women, especially one Martha Simmons and some others, under pretence of some divine motions, grew somewhat turbulent, and interrupting the ministry and service of the said F. Howgill and E. Burrough in some public meetings, interrupting the public service wherein ... F.H. and E.B. were engaged. Whereupon the said Martha and another woman [possibly Hannah Stranger] went and made their complaint to James Nayler ... endeavouring to set him against them and to draw judgement against them from him.[35]

Nayler did not meet Martha Simmons' request, perhaps out of a reluctance to split the movement. Furthermore, he had a close tie with Howgill[36] with whom he had been imprisoned at Appleby and who had described Nayler as being like a father to him. Whatever his reasons were they did not prevent Martha from falling into a fit of weeping and reproaching him for his lack of co-operation. Nayler was acutely distressed by her response to such an extent that he became, according to Whitehead:

Clouded in his understanding, bewildered and at a loss for judgement. Thus (poor man) he stood not in his dominion (as he should have done) over that dividing, false transforming spirit [Martha Simmons] which sought to sow discord among brethren; which for a time caused some estrangement and distance in him from his brethren and true friends.[37]

What appears to have happened is that the Friends, seeing Nayler changed from the charismatic figure he had been previously, who as Martha herself later said 'had overcome all the priests who came to him and others,' felt Martha had exerted a malignant influence over him; some accused her of witchcraft. She asserted her innocence from that point onwards: '... they all concluded that I had bewitched him, when alas I was as innocent as a child.'[38] What happened next seems to have been a closing of Quaker ranks against her. Nayler could not circulate among the Friends as before. The exact reasons are not clear but he would seem to have been in a kind of catatonic depression, which disabled him, and the people came to Martha's house and took him away. Nayler went to Bristol where Martha followed him and both attended a Meeting for worship but Nayler remained silent. After the Meeting a rather bizarre event seems to have taken place in which Nayler led the group to a house by the orchard. The others followed and according to Martha's account, they were 'used very sorely.' Afterwards they went to the home of Dennis Hollister and Henry Row who were friends of Nayler and his associates but they were followed and ill-treated. Martha related these incidents as taking place 'about twelve weeks since,' meaning before they were arrested and therefore in August 1656.

Martha went to another Meeting and after a period of silence stood up, condemned the Friends saying there was not one who would take her part and began to chant the words, 'Innocency, Innocency' for over an hour. Richard Hubberthorne was also at the Meeting and later wrote that:

When we had waited in silence a while, she stood up and spoke, judging all Friends that they were not come to the cross ... And then she fell on singing, with an unclean spirit. And the substance of that which she said in her singing was, Innocency, innocency, innocency, many times over, for the space of one hour or more, but in the power of the Lord I was moved to speak soon after she begun ... then, she was tormented against me, and cried of deep subtlety, for a long time together, turning it into a song, and that we were all the beast, and I the head of the beast ...[39]

On 1st August 1656 Nayler set out to travel to Launceston with the intention of visiting Fox and perhaps repairing some of the damage done to the movement by their disagreements in London. Martha returned to London and in September secured work as a nurse to the wife of Major General Desborough, Oliver Cromwell's brother-in-law.[40] Nayler did not arrive in Launceston but was arrested while passing through Exeter and word was sent to Martha. She began to negotiate Nayler's release to which Cromwell eventually agreed and in October 1656 signed the warrant. Martha and Thomas Simmonds travelled almost straightaway to Exeter and on 20th October Nayler was released. Thomas returned directly to London and it seems he tried to persuade Martha to do likewise but to no avail. She remained with Nayler along with Timothy Wedlock,[41] Hannah Stranger, and Dorcas Erbury who set out for Glastonbury on foot. Historians have focused on the event in Bristol, perhaps because it is the most well-documented and the one for which he was punished but what has rarely been given attention is the fact that they performed the same sign at Glastonbury and Wells. George Witherley's[42] evidence during Nayler's examination also supports this:

> Nayler ... had been not long released out of Exeter Gaol, ... and [Nayler, Simmons, Dorcas Erbury, Timothy Wedlock, Hannah Stranger] were ... intended for London; but must it seems come this way to play their pranks with us, [a]s well as in other places as they past through: For at Wells and Glastonbury his [ac]complices strewed their garments in the way of this Imposter Nailer.

The party travelled from Wells to Glastonbury and then on to Bristol through the small village of Bedminster where they encountered George Witherley. It was by all accounts 'rainy and foul weather' and the party travelling bareheaded along the cartway were apparently oblivious to the mud and dirt in which they were walking. A marginal note to Witherley's evidence reads: 'it was exceeding wet weather, the Spouts on the Bridge (which is a narrow place) poured on his barehead so that it ran out at his knees.' This seems to have aroused some anger in Witherley who reproached them saying that God did not require such a sign. In this way they finally arrived at the Ratcliffe Gate of Bristol on the Friday, 24th October 1656. Thomas Wedlock led the party on foot and the two women, Martha Simmons and Hannah Stranger[43] led Nayler's horse with the reins in their hands, one on each side singing 'holy, holy, holy' and spreading their clothing on the earth before him in a prophetic re-enactment of Christ's entry into Jerusalem. Dorcas Erbury[44] followed the party. They travelled in this way to the High Cross of Bristol (the preaching cross) and from there to an inn called The White Hart in Broadstreet, the home of two other eminent Quakers, Dennis Hollister and Henry Row. By this time the city magistrates had been informed and all seven of them were sent to appear before them. Again the evidence of George Witherley tells us that:

> Two women were leading the said James Nailer, with the reins in their hand; one of each side, ... who came singing, Holy, holy, holy, Lord God of Israel. And in this posture he rode to the high Crosse of Bristol; and from thence to the White Hart in Broadstreet ... singing, Hosanna, and holy, holy etc.[45]

The Evidence

The whole party was arrested the same day and appeared before the Bristol magistrates on the following day, Saturday, 25th October. Nayler answered the questions shrewdly or remained silent to avoid incriminating himself. When asked why they went before him singing he replied by saying they were of an age to speak for themselves.[46] When asked whether or not his name was Jesus he gave no answer nor did he say anything at all about the name Jesus being applied to him. They were all very guarded in their replies, almost to the extent that we could think their words had been rehearsed. In a sense this was true, as they had almost all been imprisoned and questioned on previous occasions. Martha was asked why she went before Nayler leading his horse and she replied by saying that she knew no James Nayler, for he had passed to a more pure estate, and the power of the Lord had impelled her to lead his horse. She says he (Nayler) is buried in her; he has died to the carnal self: 'he has promised to come a second time: he will be reborn as the spiritual body of Christ.'[47] When Dorcas Erbury was asked how Nayler could be Jesus who was crucified on a cross, she replied: 'he is manifested in him.' Nowhere in the course of questioning could any one of the accused be found guilty of a belief, *per se,* in the divinity of Nayler. Hannah Stranger was perhaps the shrewdest and must have infuriated the examining magistrate by repeating, 'If you have anything against me' several times. Thomas Stranger acted similarly, he said little and refused to answer most of the questions put to him. He did, however, admit to the crucial piece of evidence, which finally convicted Nayler: a post-script to a letter written by his wife to Nayler. The party had been searched on arrest and a number of letters found on them. The first letter mentioned in the account of their examinations was from one Jane Woodcock, about whom we are told only that she is a 'wife.' The letters had presumably been sent to Nayler during his term in prison but his reason for carrying them are obscure, for they were the incriminating evidence of his blasphemy. It has been argued that Nayler actually courted martyrdom,[48] in which case he purposely took the letters for they all address him in christological terms, but we can only surmise. Woodcock's letter referred to him as 'the Prophet of the most high' and another letter written by Martha to William Dewsbury, opens with the words, 'Oh let me for evermore be tried by the hands of Jesus.' This was incriminating but the crucial letter was one from Hannah Stranger to Nayler, in which she addresses Nayler as, 'thou everlasting son of Righteousness and Prince of Peace,' to which Thomas Stranger had added a postscript referring to Nayler as: 'no more James but Jesus.' Nayler was sent to Newgate prison accompanied by Martha and by Hannah Stranger. The ending of this dramatic sign took place in Newgate Prison, on the 25th October after the prisoner had been committed. According to Cole, a prison keeper, Nayler was visited by Martha Simmons and Hannah Stranger who, on their departure, knelt down before Nayler who placed his hands on their heads and made 'a groaning noise within himself.[49] As the women rose he clasped his hands on a cross and held it over their heads and then as they rose he spread his hands over their heads and they departed. The date is corroborated in the evidence of Thomas Perkins, a prisoner for debt in Newgate who spoke at Nayler's trial on 11th November and he describes it as being, '25 of *October* last or thereabouts.' Nayler was re-examined 'in the Painted Chamber of

Westminster, before the Committee of Parliament, the 25th November 1656.'[50] He was accused of encouraging his entourage to regard him as Christ and charged with blasphemy in a trial, which lasted ten days and ended on 16th December. The House considered what his punishment should be, if not death and it was decided:

> That on Thursday next, 18th December he stand in the pillory, the New Palace Yard, with a paper of his offence and crime in his Breast. And then presently to be whipped by the Hangman, to the Old Exchange upon *Saturday* following, to be put in the Pillory for two hours, before the exchange; and then bored through the tongue with a hot iron, and stigmatised with the letter 'B' on his forehead: And afterwards, be by the Sheriffs of London, conveyed to Bristol and there ride through the City on a horse, with his face to the horse's tail, and then publicly whipped through the town: and then by the Sheriffs of Bristol, to be conveyed to Bridewell in London and to be there kept prisoner from all society of People, from pen ink and paper, kept to hard labour and to eat no more than he earns from his labour, and not to be released until further order from Parliament.[51]

Like the two women who stood at the foot of the Cross at the Crucifixion, Martha and Hannah Stranger stood on either side of Nayler throughout the administration of his punishment thereby completing their apocalyptic re-enactment of the cross. They were also imprisoned but were released after a short time while Nayler remained in the dreadful conditions of the Bridewell Prison.

Finale

In spite of the tragic consequences for James Nayler, who initially was physically and spiritually crushed by his punishment, the women involved with him seem to have found it an empowering experience. Martha continued to interrupt meetings with even greater zeal. Richard Hubberthorne reported to Margaret Fell[52] that Martha enacted a Eucharist in which bread and wine were broken and distributed. She also read some words from Ezekiel, saying: 'that the Lord had sent that chapter to be read unto us.' Perhaps she spoke the words of Ezekiel 2.3-4:

I send thee to the children of Israel, to a rebellious nation that hath rebelled against me ... For they are impudent children and stiff hearted. I do send thee unto them.

It is demonstrable from Martha's texts that the re-enactment of Christ's 'adventus' into Jerusalem was taking place metaphorically as early as 1655[53] and in fact was a kind of subtext to all her activity within the Quaker movement. Its final, public re-enactment was the culmination of a stream of events in Martha's belief and ministry.

During her cross-examination in Bristol jail Martha was asked why she sang before James Nayler and she replied by saying:

I know not James Nayler. He was but now is past to a more pure estate, and the power of the Lord carried me to sing and lead his horse ... when the new life shall be borne in *James Nailer,* then he will be *Jesus.*[54]

It is a difficult reply in which she struggles to express the complex belief in re-birth through conversion, the 'new life' equating with the indwelling presence of Jesus and thereby participating in the life of Jesus. She did not however believe him to be the re-incarnate Christ in a traditional Protestant theological sense, but believed that Christ was present in him through the 'new life.' The evidence implies that this was how Nayler saw himself for in his examination he was asked categorically: 'Have any called thee by the name of Jesus?' to which he replied, 'not as unto the visible, but as Jesus, the Christ that is in me.' This is akin to the widespread Quaker belief that there is something of God, something divine, in all people of all races, ages and genders.

The Aftermath

In 1658 Nayler was reunited with the mainstream Quakers and died in King's Repton shortly after his release from prison. He was walking north towards his Yorkshire family and farm and left timeless words beginning 'I know a spirit that delights to do no evil'. It is not known exactly when Martha became reconciled with the orthodox Quakers, nor indeed, is much of her life known after this event. In 1657 she seems to have spent some time in Salisbury[55] but if she remained steadfast in her loyalty to Nayler his reconciliation might have persuaded her to follow and do likewise. Nothing is known of the last years of her life but it can be assumed that if

24

she remained at the Bull and Mouth her life would not have been an easy one. As early as 1655 the Oath of Abjuration which required all to prove they were not Catholic caused anxiety for the Quakers, many of whom were imprisoned for refusing to swear, but after the Restoration of 1662 the persecution of Quakers was carried out with increased zeal. In 1662 the Act of Parliament against Friends and the Conventicle Act of 1664 made it illegal for more than four people to gather for worship outside the established church. This resulted in widespread persecution with two main targets being the Horsleydown Meeting at Southwark and the Bull and Mouth:

> The last First day as innocently as ever Friends kept their usual meetings; and about the tenth hour came the life-guard with their headpieces and breast-pieces, and in Cheapside they remained; and the trained band-men they came to the Bull [Bull and Mouth meeting house] and laid hold of all the Friends they could, which were very many; some were carried on their muskets to prison and some very much beaten and abused ...[56]

The accounts of Martha's death are contradictory apart from agreement on the year of 1665. Zaller and Greaves record her death as being en route to Maryland in 1665. Kenneth Carroll quotes records of her death: the burial records of the London and Middlesex Quarterly Meeting state that she died on 27th September, 1665 and was buried the same day. Another source records her death at sea on 7th April 1665, again en route to Maryland.[57] Hannah Stranger had already reconciled herself with mainstream Quakerism and emigrated to Maryland after the death of her husband. Thomas Simmonds most probably predeceased Martha if she left for Maryland, as it is unlikely that she would have left him to run the business alone. There is no record of any children of Martha and Thomas Simmonds. The last imprint with the Bull and Mouth was in 1662; the building was destroyed by fire in 1666 and its records destroyed with it. Giles Calvert died in August 1663 and his widow Elizabeth Calvert took over the business until her death in 1674. The Quaker side of the work had already been handed over to Thomas Simmonds around 1656/7 but little else is known of him. His last imprint was in 1662 and we can presume his death took place then or shortly afterwards and by the beginning of the eighteenth century, there was no one by either name active in the London book trade.[58]

NOTES

1. Much of the following information regarding the Calvert's family background is found in Edward Thomas, *A Purveyor of Soul-Poysons, An Analysis of the Career of Giles Calvert, A Publisher and Bookseller in Mid-Seventeenth Century London*, Doctoral Thesis, La Trobe University, Australia, 1999, ch. 1.
2. Somerset County Archives, Meare Parish Records.
3. Meare Parish Records, Somerset Record Office.
4. Meare Parish Records, Somerset Record Office.
5. Somerset County Archives, Marriage Licences for Diocese of Wells, D/D/01 18, p.94.
6. Two other sons named Giles and George had died in 1613 and 1619 but it was not uncommon for a child to be named after a deceased sibling.
7. Somerset Archive and Record Service, D/D/Cd 34, Diocese of Wells Deposition Books 1602.
8. Edward Thomas, p.35.
9. Edward Thomas suggests this theory but there is no documentary evidence.
10. There are no entries in the Meare Parish Register for her death or marriage.
11. Edward Thomas, ch. 1.
12. For a detailed description of the seventeenth-century English Parish, see Anthea Jones, *A Thousand Years of the English Parish*, London: Windrush Press, 2000.
13. John Collinson, *The History and Antiquities of the County of Somerset, collected from authentick records, and an actual survey made by the late Mr. Edmumd Rack* 3 vols., Bath: R. Crutwell, 1791.
14. Martha Simmons, *A Lamentation for the Lost Sheep of the House of Israel*, 11, 165-167, 177-179.
15. In 1656 Martha would have been thirty three years old. If the fourteen year period was immediately prior to the publication of *A Lamentation* in 1656 it covered her years between the ages of nineteen and thirty three. If we take the figure fourteen to an approximation then her arrival in London would have been between 1636-1640.
16. Marginal note in 'The Examination of Martha Symonds,' in *A True Narrative of the Examination, Tryall and Sufferings of James Nayler*, p.28.
17. For a complete list of Giles Calvert's imprints see Appendices, 1&2, Edward Thomas' thesis.
18. The most significant and influential was Jacob Bohme (1575-1624) whose two most influential works were *The Great Mystery* and *On the Election of Grace*.

19. The reasons for this interest in European spiritual writing is complex but the effect of the Thirty Years War was one of the circumstances out of which the desire for spiritual renewal emerged.

20. George Fox, *Journal*, ch. 8, p.99.

21. Douglas Gwyn, *Seekers Found, Atonement in Early Quaker Experience*, Pennsylvania: Pendle Hill, 2000, p.245.

22. William Crouch, 'Postuma Christiana', 1712, quoted in George W. Edwards, 'The Bull and Mouth Meeting House, its Site and Environs,' *The Friends Quarterly*, 9, 1955, pp.78-84.

23. Although the spellings for both Martha and Thomas Simmon(d)s vary, Simmonds is the form used most often for Thomas.

24. James Nayler's Examination, in *The Grand Imposter Examined: or The Life, Tryal, and Examination of James Nayler, The Seduced and Seducing Quaker with the Manner of his Riding into Bristol*, printed for Henry Brome, London, 1656, p.3.

25. Accounts of Nayler's date of birth vary from 1615 to 1619.

26. Leo Damrosch, *The Sorrows of the Quaker Jesus*, Cambridge (Massachusetts): Harvard University Press, 1996, p.116.

27. 1 Cor. 1: 11-13.

28. Edward Thomas, p.35.

29. Alexander Parker to Margaret Fell, 21st July, 1655, *Swarthmore MSS* 1: 62, quoted in Edward Thomas, p.150.

30. H. J. Cadbury (ed.) *Letters to William Dewsbury and Others* published as monograph in 22, 1948 and quoted in Kenneth Carroll, 'Martha Simmonds, A Quaker Enigma,' *Journal of Friends Historical Society*, 53, 1972, pp.31-52.

31. *A True Narrative, p.*10.

32. *A True Narrative*, pp.10, 11.

33. Cadbury, *Letters to William Dewsbury and Others*.

34. Braithwaite, *Beginnings of Quakerism*, pp.155-164.

35. George Whitehead, (ed.) *A Collection of Sundry Books, Epistles and Papers, Written by James Nayler, Some of which were never printed before Printed. With an Impartial Relation to His Life*, London, 1712.

36. Francis Howgill, was one of the first Quaker leaders to be converted by George Fox in Sedburgh in 1652. In 1654 Howgill initiated the preaching campaign with Edward Burrough in London.

37. George Whitehead, *Collection of Sundry Books*, (by James Nayler) quoted in Damrosch, p.116.

38. *A True Narrative*, p.11.

39. Letter of 26th July 1656, quoted by Carroll, 'A Quaker Enigma,' p.40.

40. Desborough was chosen by Cromwell to organise local government from 1655 until 1657.

reprinted with her second text, *A Lamentation for the Lost Sheep of Israel*. *A Lamentation* is a pamphlet of six pages published by her brother, Giles Calvert, on 16th October 1655. It was reprinted the following year with the text of the earlier broadsheet as the second part of the pamphlet. We have further evidence for the date of this text from the inscription on the Thomason tract: *20 October 1655*. The last work ascribed to Martha Simmons is a multi-authored pamphlet in which she, Hannah Stranger,[2] James Nayler and William Tomlinson[3] seek to address the spiritual crisis of the age and to justify the sign re-enacted at Bristol. The pamphlet, which has no title page, is known as *O England thy time is come*, as these are the opening words of the short introduction by James Nayler. It contains three tracts by Martha Simmons, one each by Hannah Stranger, William Tomlinson, another by Nayler and concludes with lines of verse composed by Nayler. The first and longest tract in the pamphlet is by Martha Simmons, *You Foolish Virgins* (Text A) of 3,246 words. *How Excellent is Thy Waies* (Text B) and *Oh My Beloved* (Text C) are her two shorter pieces of 839 and 840 words respectively. The absence of an imprint makes the dating of *O England* difficult but there are sufficient, albeit elliptical, references to the Bristol event on 24th October 1656 for us to assume it to have been written after this date. The Thomason tract copy has a handwritten calculation on the cover, subtracting 1659-1604[4] which possibly suggests that it was being circulated in 1659. It also contains a short piece presumably written by Nayler during his imprisonment: *A Morning-Song when I being in Prison in Westminster*. Nayler was taken before Magistrates on Saturday, 25th October 1656[5] and was sentenced in November 1656. In December 1656 Martha Simmons was in prison[6] and so we could assume the text to have been published after that date although parts of it may have been written earlier. It was most likely to have been published by either Giles Calvert or Thomas Simmonds who had taken over most of the Quaker side of Giles Calvert's publications. The most reliable evidence for ascertaining the date of this text is the internal evidence obtained from a reading of the text, which I hope to demonstrate.

There are a number of considerations to be taken into account in evaluating these writings. Firstly, it is important to take into account the intensely biblical nature of seventeenth-century culture with its apocalyptic focus on the imminent return of Christ as supreme ruler. Secondly, an understanding of the texts is possible only if read within the context of what can be reconstructed of Martha Simmons' own life. Thirdly, her texts, preaching and occasional enactment of 'signs' were the expressions of a total persona, which cannot be identified solely through the texts.

When the Lord Jesus came to Jerusalem

The most outstanding feature of Martha Simmons' first composition is its similarity to the New Testament structure of the Matthean and Johannine texts. The gospel of Matthew is shaped around a series of discourses or sermons preceded by short narrative episodes or vignettes, which provide the material for the sermon. The first of these is the Matthean ethic of the kingdom (ch. 5-7) followed by a discourse on the nature of mission within an eschatological context. This is followed by the discourse on the nature and coming of the kingdom in a series of what C.H. Dodd describes as the 'kingdom parables'. They are particularly significant for two reasons: they occur in Matthew's gospel immediately after Christ's triumphal entry into Jerusalem, the starting point of Martha Simmons narrative, and before his arrest and Crucifixion.

The opening lines of *When the Lord Jesus* might seem chillingly prophetic when read in the light of later events and it is not too implausible to suggest that Martha had made a highly personal reading of Matt. 21, the biblical preface to the description of Christ's entry into Jerusalem:

> Tell ye the daughter of Si-on, 'Behold, thy King cometh unto thee, meek, and sitting upon an ass, and a colt the foal of an ass.[7]

Martha Simmons, however, was not unique in using the motif of Jesus entering Jerusalem on Palm Sunday; it was the ultimate icon of eschatology among the millenarian sects who firmly believed that they were living at the end of the one thousand years referred to in the Book of Revelation.[8] For the sects the question of salvation and all its associated anxieties was uppermost in religious discourse. Their spirituality was intrinsically both eschatological and soteriological and therefore concerned with the concept of and exploration of finality with all its possible implications. This image is followed by a series of warnings with allusions to the eschatological gospels; the text is already in a specifically theological framework. Futhermore, the parables selected for these admonitions or

31

warnings are specifically those of Matt. 21 and 25 and it is worth looking at how these chapters have been worked into the text as Martha uses them again and in greater detail in her two later works.

The first allusion is to the parable of the steward and talents,[9] which is blended with the Genesis narrative of Adam and Eve and the Garden of Eden. The steward who returns (ll.13-14) is God and the narrative returns to the Old Testament account of creation[10] with Adam's awareness of his nakedness being used as an analogy for the fallen state of England. The Garden of Eden is then linked to the New Testament (1.26,30) when the parable of the wedding feast is introduced.[11] The man who arrives without a wedding garment is cast into the outer darkness just as Adam and Eve were cast out of the presence of God:

> there is a Talen to be improved in thee, how wilt thou give an accompt of it; the Steward is now come: in the coole of the day, then Adam heard the voyce of God, and then he saw his nakednese, and so mayest thou; If thou wilt turn in thy minde to the light of Christ in thee, the light will discover to thee thy fallen state, and how thou art turned out from the presence of God, and art in the gall of bitternesse, and the earth is cursed for thy sake ... (ll.13-18)

What then happens is a return to the Old Testament through the introduction of another parable, that of the wedding feast.[12] What links this to the earlier parable is the final casting into darkness of the man who arrived without the cloak. Although the full narrative of the steward distributing the talents is not narrated here it also ends with the foolish servant who had used his talent unwisely being cast out into the darkness.

At this stage a pattern is beginning to emerge of images and themes from Old and New Testaments being juxtaposed to create time shifts which allow Martha to present herself as an integral part of the overall biblical story: Jesus weeps and laments over Jerusalem but she cannot mourn over the people (1.1-4).[13] The faithful and unfaithful servants,[14] sheep and goats,[15] the unforgiving servant and the wise employer all end in the final separation of one from the other. The narrative moves between the Old and New Testaments to demonstrate a particular point about time. Time is crucial in all her writings from the beginnings of time (Adam and Eve) to the end of time (the second coming of Christ). The purpose of this shift from Old to New Testament is made clear (1.35) when she says:

> Now Christ Jesus the second Adam, who is God, manifest in the flesh, condemning sinne in the flesh, if thou live in him in thee, and believe in hime in thee, then thou wilt witnesse his power to the cutting down of thy will ... (ll.35-37)

i.e. the New Testament is read as the fulfilment of the Old and final age; the Parousia is already here through the indwelling of Christ in every man and woman if they will only believe and submit to his will. But this is not the only way in which the question of apocalypse is developed. Images of death and the end of time recur particularly at this point (ll.15-20); birth and death, meeting of light and darkness (ll.40-43).

The concept of Christ indwelling in all people is an expression of the fundamental Quaker belief in the 'inner light' by which true redemption is found. It was a phrase originally used by George Fox to describe his conversion and became a fundamental principle of Quaker belief and part of the theological battle in which they struggled to justify their beliefs, here emphasised by the words, 'the light of Christ in thee' (1.16) and 'a measure of Christ' (1.50). The light should not be confused with conscience or reason; but an expression of the Quaker belief that God dwelt intrinsically in all people allowing human beings an immediate sense of God's presence and will for them.

This is followed by the biblical narrative of the wandering prophets of the Old Testament (ll.93-101), concluding with a reference to Christ 'who had no abiding place,' an image to which she returns in her later text and possibly indicates something of her own experience.

A Lamentation for the Lost Sheep of the House of Israel

The two biblical texts on the title page introduce the themes of the second pamphlet, an admonition to the people of England to repent:

> I have seen also in the Prophets of Jerusalem a horrible thing, they commit adultery, and walke in lies; they strengthen also the hand of evill doers, that none doth return from his

wickednesse; they are all of them unto me as Sodom, and the inhabitants thereof as Gomorah. (Jer. 23.14)

and a heralding of the kingdom:

> Awake, awake put on thy strength O Sion, put on thy beautiful garments O Jerusalem, the holy City, for henceforth there shall no more come unto thee the uncircumcised and the unclean. (Is. 52).

Thematically therefore this second text is a development of her first publication, *When the Lord Jesus*, but, more complex in terms of structure, and more specific in the presentation of her spiritual development and theologically more developed in her model of scriptural interpretation. New themes such as anticlericalism and a model of scripture, which had not been discussed previously, and which suggest the direction of her spiritual development, here become more clearly defined. Seeking was a common contemporary identity with complex social origins, arising from the spiritual chaos and social injustices of the Civil War. It was also a metaphor for seeking the kingdom, the New Jerusalem whose coming many people believed to be imminent.

Seeking in this text develops along three channels. Firstly (ll.1-68) a relatively short section develops the introductory reference to Jeremiah on the title page, i.e., the fallen state of the nation and the calls for repentance balanced by the development of the text from Isaiah, which describes the joys of the kingdom. This is composed of biblical paraphrases and references to the kingdom parables with many images of being lost and searching. The next section attempts to develop this theme by providing an explanation for the loss, of why they cannot 'finde the doore to enter the kingdom' (l.73) which is partially because they have been misled by the clergy and institutional church. They have neither discovered the 'inner light' nor understood the true nature of the 'word' and this is crucial to her spirituality. Finally, seeking takes on a personal note with Martha's own account of her spiritual and personal seeking and conversion and her eventual 'resting place.'

The text opens with the characteristic seeker image of 'stumbling and groping' (2)[16] followed immediately by a reference to 'high' things. This is a recurring image and important to Quaker spirituality. The Quakers had a deep-rooted fear and mistrust of what they described as 'high and lofty' things, by which they meant

34

intellectual and social achievement and the aspiration for such, as well as its being a pejorative term for the established clergy who preached from pulpits. Another thing it implied was anything carnal, 'the arm of flesh and the multitude of thy conceivings' (24-21). These were the things that put 'stumbling blocks' before the truth. Therefore to be grown so 'high in thy fallen wisdom' was to be spiritually lost and this is central to Martha Simmons' works which are her own account of her spiritual seeking and finding, expressed so appropriately by the image of the Pearl. One of the striking aspects of all her works is her fundamental sense of hope in human nature: unlike some of her contemporaries, she never makes an outright condemnation or expression of despair She appropriates biblical expressions of hope, reminding the people of the fundamental goodness within them with phrases like the 'Royal Diadem' (1.9) within them, and the 'inward eye,' which is waiting to be opened. This kind of language is not unique to Martha Simmons: Ann Gargill, also a London Quaker whose works were published by Giles Calvert, uses the same imagery when she describes God as: 'a diadem of Gold; a Sceptre of Righteousness.'[17]

Throughout this section we have the powerful image of being trapped, the 'soule in death' (1.13) the 'horrible pit' (1.17) and of one's goal being just beyond reach. The true nature of that goal is compared with the fragility of human nature (ll. 19-28), but strength is born from submission, bending 'thy necke to the yoak of Christ'. That human strength and wisdom are in fact the power of God working through the human is derived essentially from Pauline teachings.[18] This section concludes with a description of the Quaker conversion experience (ll.39-68), which is introduced with what she terms a 'war ... contrary to thy will.' This refers to the spiritual struggle, undergone in the process of seeking, a struggle which one must accept passively to allow the 'light' to dwell in the soul. If one rejects this (ll.46-47) then the light will be withdrawn and given to another (1.52). At this point (1.69) Martha addresses the clergy in terms very similar to the opening lines: 'teachers of all sorts of opinions', who have been 'groping and hunting' (ll.70-71), in search of the precious pearl but the language now becomes much more specifically targeted than earlier as she is introducing two crucial themes in reply to the questions raised at the beginning: the corruption of the clergy and the misinterpretation of scripture. She is forthright in her address to the clergy (ll.81-83) and develops this attack to try to define the true nature of the individual with God. The Quakers had two fundamental objections to the stipendiary clergy: if the essence of God dwelt intrinsically in all creatures then the priests and sacraments were superfluous as mediators between God and the individual soul. Their second objection was to the payment of tithes and clergy stipends. They believed the word of God should be free to all, a belief derived from Revelation 17. To demand payment was 'stealing from your neighbour' (81). She also condemns them for their persecution of the Quakers, 'raising up false accusations against the children of Light and those that walk in it' (87-88). She had been at one stage of her ministry imprisoned in Colchester for 'speakeing to a priest.'[19]

Immediately the theme of light is introduced she moves to another fundamental Quaker belief, the doctrine of the inner light and its relationship with scripture and the complex theological concept of the logocentric nature of God. This was a belief that the voice of God spoke through those who attended to the inner light; the scriptures were the documented accounts of such, but not the voice of God *per se.* It was the main source of contention between the Quakers and the other Puritan groups and the Church of England who all believed the scriptures to be the definitive word of God. When we look at the last section in this context, it becomes possible to see the account of the 'true priests,' the wandering prophets of the Old Testament, as opening a debate on the nature of religious authority and the right to preach.

A Lamentation concludes her attacks on the clergy (ll.141-197) with a tremendous sense of urgency and with a call to repentance. The Quakers not only modelled their lives and faith on what they perceived to be the ethos of the early Church, but like the first apostles, she firmly believed that the Risen Christ would return very soon. Like the early Christian communities, she also believed that they were personally united with Christ and that they were living in the end times and seeing life in polarised terms of good and evil, life and death, heaven and hell. Emphasis on a personal and individual faith meant abandoning the idea that a collective body such as the Church could control the union of the soul with God. 'Him in me' (35) was the unnegotiated, unconditional dwelling of God within the soul through faith and rejection of material excesses and of one's own desires, 'for thy will must come to death.' The Quakers objected to the mediating institutions of the church and sacraments especially Baptism and the Eucharist.

Finally she gives an account of her own searching (1.163) and wandering through the streets of London in search of an 'honest minister' which she finds eventually within herself, in the 'glimmerings of light', which is the word of God within her. It is very similar to George Fox's account of his conversion recorded many years later in which he also describes years of searching in vain. Finally, she sees the light as 'something groaning within me,' (1.183) and she also tells us when she found what she had been searching for: 'about the end of the last seven years the Lord opened my eyes' (ll.185-6). She concludes on a prophetic note to which she returns in one of her later tracts of *O England:* 'and this is my beloved and this is my friend, O daughters of Jerusalem' (ll.191-192).

O England; thy time is come (Texts A, B, C)

Multiple authorship and the absence of an imprint combine to create a difficulty in establishing both the dates of individual compositions and of the publication of the pamphlet. We can deduce from its themes of apocalypse and valediction that it was written after the entry into Bristol in 1656.

A short section by James Nayler prefaces the pamphlet:

> Oh England thy time is come, God hath not taken
> Thee until thou be ful: yea the fullness of thy time
>   is come;
> With speed prepare to meet the Lord in Judgement,
>   lest thou be cut off:
> wo unto thee if he turn from thee before thou
> Be refined. Remember, was not the Jewes cut off
>   that thou
> Might be grafted in? Remember and take heed (Ll.1-6)

Apocalypse, admonition, eschatology are all repeated here. The cryptic reference to 'the Jewes,' does not imply anti-Semitism but reflects the radical protestant identity with the Old Testament Israelites. If the chronological dating of this text is not immediately obvious we can deduce from the highly apocalyptic opening biblical quotation[20] that theologically this is a 'post Resurrection' text. In the two earlier texts we follow the narrative through the arrival of Christ into Jerusalem, an event re-enacted in the Bristol entry.

The consequences of that act precipitated the 'sign of the Cross' when Martha and Hannah Stranger stood to the right and left of Nayler as witnesses to the brutality of his punishment. The final days of Revelation have arrived; 'yea, the fulness of thy time is come' and it is within this framework that we must approach it and read the reference to the Ascension as an indication that whatever theological conflict had been at the heart of Martha Simmons' quest it had in some way been resolved. The aim of the pamphlet seems to be to place the Bristol event in a particular biblical and theological context, thereby categorising it as the will and command of God. In an earlier text of 1655 James Nayler had written:

> What we doe, is not from the command that was to others, nor herein do we walke by Tradition, but from command of the same power, by which we are sent forth.[21]

Unlike Martha's two earlier publications, the tone of O *England* is not essentially admonitory (although there are elements of that) but judgmental. In *A Lamentation* the foolish virgins were being warned to stay awake but here they are rebuked for having fallen asleep and the change of tense, the sense of 'before and after', links it inextricably to the Bristol event.

> This glorious Reign of Christ is come;
> Ho! everyone behold the Sonne:
> This is the beautiful Morning-Star.

If the two earlier texts were written as warnings, here she is quite clear about the question with the reminder: 'Thou hast not wanted for warnings.' The second and third texts of O *England* by Martha Simmons, beginning, *How Excellent is thy Ways* and O *My Beloved* (texts B and C), differ from A in so far as they are the expressions of a private self written as meditations. The reason for this change may be found in Text A where she asks, 'What yet shall I say' (1.43) which has the sense of an approaching end and suggests that she perhaps saw her mission as completed by Bristol and following events. The time for warnings is over and Martha Simmons justifies her condemnation with a reminder of the warnings she has previously given in her travels, writings and enactments. The imagery of O *England* bears many similarities to that of *A Lamentation*, and she actually refers directly to this text with a plea:

> in thy Cities, Towns, and Market-Streets, I have past with bitter cryes and streams of tears, for a[ll] most two yeers

time, warning you of this day that is coming upon you as a Snare, with this Lamentation ... (ll.12-15)

but it is a far more powerful piece of writing with imagery which is both more violent and final than that of the earlier texts. In *When the Lord Jesus* she urged:

> And if thou take diligent heed to this light in thee, thou shalt finde it checking thee continually for all thy evill deeds, and it will teach thee to be sober minded and upright in all thy dealings as in the light of God: and so thou wilt come to see the straight gate and narrow way that leads to life. (ll.20-32)

and in the *Lamentation* she is compassionate:

> and the further we follow him in the straight gate and narrow way, we see that his love is past finding out: And now in the tendernesse of my heart longing for your soules good am I made open to you ... (ll.161-164)

In *O England* we see that her biblical imagery is much more forthright and even violent, drawing heavily on the images of retributive justice of the Old Testament:

> Thou art fat and full, thou art fitted for slaughter,[22] and great and terrible will thy day of calamity be; the Sword[23] of the Lord is drawn against thee, and will be sheathed in thy bowels.[24] O repent! repent, and let the destruction of Sodom[25] be a warning to thee O England! fitted for slaughter ... (ll.24-28)

Blood imagery recurs throughout the first section of this text:

> nothing will satisfie but blood; yea, yea the time is come that nothing will satisfie but blood: Thou art making thy self drunken with the blood of the Innocent; he will be a-venged of thee; till blood come up to the Horses bridle; thou art making thy self drunken with the blood of the innocent, and now he will give thee blood to drink. (ll.31-38)

and as so frequently elsewhere she moves adeptly from the Old to New Testaments the 'blood of the Innocent' becomes the 'blood to the Horses Bridle'.[26] The language of this passage is particularly violent and reflects the disturbed nature of the social and political climate in which Martha moved. Beginning with a (probable) reference to the punishment meted out to Nayler for the Bristol incident ('in thee is found slain the blood of the Innocent') she moves on to expand the metaphor of blood and slaughter so that it becomes a condemnation not only of Nayler's punishment but of the treatment and rejection of all the Friends.

The second paragraph opens with a return to the slower more restrained tone of the *Lamentation*. 'This mournful cry' etc. recounts her wanderings and journeys and her cry 'How cruelly have they beaten thy prophets' (ll.53-54) reminds us of the litany of Old Testament prophets in *When the Lord Jesus*; but this is also an elliptical reference to James Nayler who she sees, symbolically, as the representation of the Risen Jesus. If this first text of *O England* were written in the early part of 1657 the punishment meted out to James Nayler would have been complete, which further suggests that her references to cruelty are related to him.

As the text develops the language becomes both increasingly apocalyptic and pointedly referential to Nayler. Scriptural references relate directly to both Nayler and Christ:

> How have you slighted the Messenger of Reconciliation? And he fulfilled all righteousness and ascended unto his father, he gave down his spirit among you ... now the Heavens are loaded with a Blessing. (ll.62-63)

We know from the quotation prefacing this text[27] that seen in the light of the 'sign' as a whole this is a 'post resurrection' text:

> And is it not more for his glory, though it be a greater cross to your wills, to purifie these bodies, and pour out the dregs thereof, than to bring down that body which was crucified at Jerusalem, seeing all one in his power and one spirit rules in both ... (ll.142-146)

Martha Simmons and her companions have been unfairly accused by both contemporaries who saw her as blasphemous and by later historians of seeing Nayler as the reality of the returned Jesus and the fulfilment, *per se* of the promised parousia but this is a naive reading of her work. This text makes it clear that she saw Nayler as a symbol of the apocalypse in which the presence of Jesus dwelt spiritually and materially. This is apparent when she says:

> This vessel is as precious to me as that which was tortured at Jerusalem ... seeing the Father hath prepared them both

... same Graces Springs from both ... Shall I not follow thee unto death O my beloved. (ll.125-128)

Her grasp of this distinction was also made clear during her examination by Bristol magistrates when she was asked:

> Quest. *Doth that Spirit of Jesus in Nailer enable him to be a Jesus to another? A.* I say there is a seed borne in him which I shall honour above all men.

In spite of the hints of regret and failure contained in the text as a whole, if we compare it to her spiritual autobiography in *A Lamentation* there is sufficient evidence to say that she had found, through her wanderings, something of what she had been seeking. Where she had earlier spoken of wandering from one minister to another, she says with a simplicity, which emerges with a sense of having personal experience:

> They are false watchmen they will smite you and bereave you of your fresh springs which you should enjoy in the Spirit, and with that which is just, judge that which is unjust and when wills would have Liberty let it be crost with the light then you will see that in your obedience you will have peace and the peace that your obedience will bring will so knit your hearts to the Lord that nothe will be too hard for you ... and this is the State of virginity ... (ll.92-97)

And this line is the key to much of what her writing is concerned with. The parable of the wise and foolish virgins weaves its way in and out of the texts to the extent that in the wider drama of the 'Marriage day' the virgins are among the key figures without any overt definition of the purpose of its repetition. Here the meaning of the imagery becomes apparent. The two motifs of Martha Simmons' writings are the Entry into Jerusalem and the Crucifixion with their associated narratives and the Coming of the Bridegroom. Virginity is Innocency, the state of the Wise Virgins, 'This is a wise Virgin ... for he that is to come is come' (ll.123,126). For Martha, Nayler symbolises both the suffering Christ and the glorified Christ (the Bridegroom). The final section of this text returns to some of the questions raised in the spiritual autobiographical section of *Lamentation* where she again laments the wandering prophets who had nowhere other than 'Caves and Dens,' but the themes of innocence and the virginity are developed in the later, shorter texts which describe her newfound peace of mind.

The first two of Martha's texts in *O England* (A and B) are separated by an apocalyptic text by Hannah Stranger on the nature of revelation, which reinforces the present fulfilment of scripture, 'how clearly the Scripture is fulfilled in our dayes,' (ll.1-2). This is expounded in a text, which identifies Nayler with the temptations of Christ 'he would have sent him Legions of Angels but he chose rather to suffer.' This is a clear reference to Nayler. The arrangement of this particular text at this point suggests that considerable care went into the pamphlet's order of collation. This text resumes where Martha finished with a plea for vigilance with the cautionary words: 'Watch, Watch, the time hasteth exceedingly, when time shall be no more.' Hannah Stranger begins with a reproach to the friends for their lack of vigilance, for their spiritual blindness: 'Consider I beseech you how clearly the Scripture is fulfilled in our days, are you not all talking of the Reign of Christ but knows it not?' Three brief discourses follow: on the nature of virginity resumed by Martha in the following text: virgins are the ones who walk in the ways of the Lord, the ones who are 'found readie to reign with Christ Jesus in righteousness, for they are diligent in the depth of the search of their own hearts, and sees how the Lord breaketh them into tendernesse.' The second discourse is on the day of the Lord, the imminent 'Reign of Christ,' and the third on the reincarnation of the Lord's chosen one whom we take to be Nayler whose sufferings are here compared to the taunts of Christ in the Garden of Gethsemane.[28] The fact that these discourses are all in one way or another taken up by Martha in her following texts suggests that the texts ascribed to Hannah Stranger, might have been co-authored with Martha.

Martha's second text of *O England* opens with four lines of verse, which immediately re-introduce the theme of virginity:

There's none can reigne with Christ but he
That is a Virgin pure in innocency.
No evil thoughts nor worc's must be,
For that will stein Virginity.

What is immediately noticeable in the second text which follows on from the first is that for the first time in any written text Martha is not addressing the reading public but God. This brief text (B) is in fact a pastiche of Psalms, particularly the opening lines (1-10) which almost paraphrase Psalm 119.33, 112; 'Teach me, O Lord, the way of thy statutes; and I shall keep it unto the end.' 'I have inclined mine heart to perform thy statutes always *even unto* the end.' We are reminded of her earlier reference to the ways of the Lord:

> ... for we that doe follow him doe finde his paths pleasant pure and sweet, and the further we follow him in the straight gate. (Lam. 11.158-160)

A short passage of Exodus follows (ll.11-16) in which she resumes the theme of her travels allegorised and presented in the biblical form of the Israelites wandering in the desert castigating the faithless who have strayed from the Lord's ways. It demonstrates perfectly the Quaker identity with Old Testament prophets and wanderers who formed the first people of God to whom the scriptures were given. The Book of Exodus is used as a paradigm for her 'seeking' and its culmination lies in her conversion and the events of Bristol. This is a short but complete narrative for it is not a text with a proselytising message but a presentation of selfhood. The central passage forms her most complete conversion statement while at the same time it acts as a reply to the questions posed in earlier texts. In *Lamentation* she had condemned the 'high Priests of this nation' (1.79) for being unable to 'finde the doore to enter into the kingdome' (1.73) but God has here 'opened a doore of Mercie to all sorts of people' (ll.23-24). The last lines introduce the next text with the reference to the 'chased Roe upon the mountains,' a reference to the *Song of Songs* which in turn reminds us of *A Lamentation* and the thematic unity of all her texts:

> ... and this is my beloved, and this is my friend, O daughters of Jerusalem. (Lam. 11.189-181)

O my Beloved is the culmination of her entire literary output. On one level it is a repetition of the same narrative contained in her first three texts, the seeking narrative in which she literally travels and wanders up and down the streets and also embarks on a spiritual journey. The kingdom parables of her earlier text are succinctly hinted at in this narrative but explicitly enough for the connection to be made. In *When the Lord Jesus* the steward asks 'how wilt thou give an accompt of it,' a question which not only forms part of the narrative of her earlier text but one she addresses to herself and here she has begun to find the answer:

43

Thou didst command me forth into thy Work to invite those in which knew thee not, and I was obedient to thee, when I returned and gave thee an account, thou didst accept my service, though men denied it, and thou gavest into my bosom a Double Blessing. (ll.8-12)

Much of the controversy surrounding Martha Simmons and James Nayler has focused on the question of whether or not she saw in Nayler the actual, as opposed to a representational reincarnation of Christ It remains a confused issue as the evidence can only be viewed in retrospect and as part of a complex theological and social situation but if we take full account of the evidence of the text alone we can say her references to Christ are in many instances clearly distinct from her references to Nayler and this seems to be something she is doing specifically and self consciously. In her letter to William Dewsbury she says she wants to be tried by the hands of Jesus, and here she says this has happened: 'Thou hast tried me, and in thy trial thou hast found me steadfast.'

She refers to her natural birth, her birth in 'this visible World' which has led her to choose death, i.e. the spiritual death which must precede the spirit becoming one with the spirit of Christ:

... I have not had pleasure in this world, but have stood as one alone; and since I knew the way to thee, I have exceedingly hasted out of it ...(ll.26-29)

This helps to contextualise her earlier references to 'birthright' (A 1.4) which means the right to a 'new birth' through conversion and thus becoming the spiritual Body of Christ through his indwelling presence. It is further endorsed when, after the eloquent description of the loneliness of her search and the joy of conversion, she says in the voice of a homecoming:

... I sought for the way to all that pretended to direct the way, but they had stoln thy words, & had not thy life so they wearied me, and profited me not; by now thou hast revealed thy son in me. Oh! How am I overcome with thy presence? and now I shall live with thee for ever. (ll.31-35)

She had, in other words, discovered the life of Christ within herself.

NOTES

1. Grigge, William, *The Quakers' Jesus*, London, 1656, p.3.
2. Hannah Stranger was a colleague of Martha Simmons and Nayler. She is described in the account of her examination, 'the wife of Thomas Stranger of London Combmaker'. James Nayler's Examination, in *The Grand Imposter Examined: or The Life, Tryal, and Examination of James Nayler, The Seduced and Seducing Quaker with the Manner of his Riding into Bristol*, printed for Henry Brome, London, 1656, p.3.
3. William Tomlinson 'WT', 1653-1696, Quaker from Wanstead in Essex, his other works are, *Seven Particulars, containeth as followeth*, 1655, *A Bosom opened to the Jewes*, 1656, *A Word of Reproof To the Priests or Ministers*, 1656, all published by Giles Calvert.
4. Possibly an attempt to calculate the age of James Nayler, although most accounts of Nayler give his dates as 1619-1660.
5. Grigge, William, *The Quakers' Jesus*, London, 1656, p.3.
6. John Deacon, *An Exact History of the life of James Nayler*, London, printed for Edward Thomas, 1657, p.49. The date of publication on the Thomason Tract has been altered from 1657 to 56, which would appear to be correct, as there is no other evidence to support her imprisonment in 1657.
7. Matt. 21, 5. John, 12, 15.
8. Rev. 20.
9. Matt. 25.15.
10. Gen. 2, 8.
11. Matt. 14.
12. Matt. 22.11
13. Gen. 3, 17.
14. Matt. 25.26.
15. Matt. 25.33.
16. Jn. 11.9-10 Deut 28.29. Also a phrase used by George Fox in a 1654 pamphlet entitled *A Warning to the World that are Groping in the Dark*, London, 1654, printed for Giles Calvert at the Sign of the Black-Spread Eagle.
17. Anne Gargill, *A Warning To all the World*, London, 1656, p.26.
18. 2 Cor. 4.6.
19. Letters to William Dewsbury.
20. Acts 1.11.
21. James Nayler, *An Answer to the Booke called the perfect Pharisee under Monkish Holinesse*, London, 1655, p.21, quoted in Kenneth L. Carroll, 'Quaker Attitudes towards Signs and Wonders,' *JFHS*, (1) 1977, pp.70-84.
22. Ezekiel, 39.19.

23. The sword in OT scripture is a symbol of the wrath of God, Gen. 27.40; Lev. 26.2; Deut. 3.41.
24. 'Bowels' in OT signify the soul. Here the Sword of the Lord has pierced the very soul of the people i.e. destroyed them.
25. Sodom and Gomorrah were the notoriously sinful cities in the Book of Genesis destroyed by 'brimstone and fire' because of their wickedness. (Gen. 19.34)
26. Blood is an image often found in Simmons texts and reflects the symbolic power the concept of bloodshed and slaughter wielded in this troubled society. Charles Stuart had been referred to as a 'man of blood' to the point where bloodshed became synonymous with the perceived injustices of his reign. See Patricia Crawford 'Charles Stuart, That Man of Blood', *Journal of British Studies*, Spring, 1977.
27. Acts 1.11
28. Matt. 26,53. 'Thinkest thou that I cannot now pray to my father and he shall presently give me more than twelve legions of angels.'

EDITORIAL NOTES TO APPENDICES

THE FOLLOWING appendices are transcripts of Martha Simmons' texts, her letter to Dewsbury and an extract of her *Examination*. The purpose of providing these is to make Martha Simmons' texts accessible to the reader, as the only surviving copies of these tracts are The Thomason Collection in the British Museum and those in the archives of Quaker institutions of North America and Britain. Most of these are only available to the general reader on microfilm. The two sources used here were the Thomason copies and those belonging to Friends' House Library, London.

In order to adhere as closely as possible to the visual presentation of the original documents only minor editorial changes have been made. The seventeenth century use of 'the long ess' and 'vv' has been altered to the modern forms of 's' and 'w' throughout, otherwise all spelling and punctuation and italicisation remain unaltered. In the case of the three published tracts the original fully justified line has been altered in favour a left justification in keeping with modern publishing preferences and line numbering has been added with the original pagination indicated internally by the use of square brackets. The transcription of *When the Lord Jesus came to Jerusalem* is based on the first edition (1655) which has evidence of its method of dissemination in the note written across the bottom of the page, presumably by Thomason himself: 'given about by the Quakers.' This has not been included, nor have such notes on the other tracts been transcribed as they do not form a part of the text *per se* and were not written by Martha Simmons.

For the second tract, *A Lamentation for the Lost Sheep of the House of Israel*, my source document was the 1655 edition with title page, as this should be read as integral to the text. The 1656 edition of this text has minor differences which amount to no more than original typographical errors being corrected, e.g. the opening line of the 1655 edition reads 'whom art thou' which has been altered to 'where' by hand. The 1656 edition reads 'where,' and in these few instances I have therefore indicated these differences by the use of square brackets. The third tract, *O England*, is also a transcription of the Thomason Tract (although the copies in Friends House in London were consulted in all cases). All reference note identifications of Biblical sources are editorial and draw attention to the deeply soteriological nature of the texts and their appropriation of scriptural imagery. All scriptural exposition is ephemeral and therefore the reference notes have attempted to give no more than 'chapter and verse' references drawn from a line by line reference carried out with the aid of Cruden's concordance.

In the case of the 'Letter to William Dewsbury' and the 'Examination of Martha Simmons' the transcripts are unaltered other than for modernising 'the long ess' and 'vv' to 's' and 'w'. Fully justified margins, and line lengths, italics and spelling have been retained. The source of these texts is Robert Rich and William Tomlinson: *A True Narrative of the Late Tryall, Sufferings and Examination of James Nayler*, 1657, the earliest account of Nayler's trial and Martha Simmons' examination. I have retained the original marginal notes, as they appear in the printed text, as these documents are self-explanatory.

Appendix One

WHEN THE LORD JESUS CAME TO JERUSALEM

When the Lord Jesus came to *Jerusalem*,[1] he beheld the City and wept over it, with this lamentation: *Oh that thou hadst known in this day the things that belong to thy peace!* The same tendernesse is witnessed now in them which the Lord hath enlightned. I cannot but mourn over you, to see how you lye wallowing in your filth, and joyne hand in hand and smite with the fist of wickednesse, and yet lean upon Christ for salvation: Know you not that *many shall say in that day, Lord, Lord?* but remember what will be your answer; *Go you cursed into the lake, I know you not.*[2] Oh that thou wouldst but stand still a little, and turn thy eye inward; Sit downe a little, and consider thy poore soul that lyes in death: What will become of thee, thou murderest the just in thee, there is a Talent to be improved in thee, how wilt thou give an accompt of it; the Steward is now come: in the coole of the day, then *Adam* heard the voyce of God, and then he saw his nakednese,[3] and so mayest thou; If thou wilt turn in thy minde to the light of Christ in thee, the light will discover to thee thy fallen state, and how thou art turned out from the presence of God, and art in the gall of bitternesse, and the earth is cursed for thy sake: Now if thou wilt minde the light, and waite in it, which is the grace of God that hath appeared to thee, there is the first step to pure redemption: And if thou take diligent heed to this light in thee, thou shalt finde it checking thee continually for all thy evill deeds, and it will teach thee to be sober minded and upright in all thy dealings as in the sight of God: and so thou wilt come to see the straight gate and narrow way that leads to life; but thou wilt say, Christ hath done all this for me, I have nothing to do but believe: but it will be said unto thee, when thou thinkest to sit downe with thy Lord; *Friend, how camest thou hither without a wedding-garment?*[4] then know what thy portion will be. Faith is another thing than thou takest it to be; He that hath Faith, if it be never so little, shall witnesse Christs words to be true, *he shall remove mountaines*: Now in the still silence, in the light that shines in darknesse in thee, thou wilt come to relish that little grain of Faith which is held in a pure conscience, and so feele the mountains remove,[5] which presseth downe thy soule: but *ye will not come unto me that ye may have life,* saith Christ Jesus; it is thy will that hinders thee, for in thy will the Devill lodges. *Adam* when he disobeyed the minde and will of God, then he entred into his own will, and so was turned out into the Devils Kingdome. Now Christ Jesus the second *Adam,* who is God manifest in flesh, condemning sinne in the flesh, if thou live in him in thee, and believe in him in thee, then thou wilt witnesse his power to the cutting down of thy will; for thy will must come to death, that the will of God may be done, and so that Scripture comes to be fulfilled in thee, which are the words of Christ; *Loe I come, in the volume of thy booke it is written of me to doe thy will O God,* which is the book of conscience in thee, there the will of God is to be done: And as thou comest to love the light, and live in it, thou wilt come to see the righteous law of God fulfilled in thee, Death reigns in thee. Now Death reigned from *Adam till Moses,*[6] and when *Moses* came, then was the Law given forth; and so *Moses* and the Prophets till *John*: But thou wilt say, *thou art not under the Law, but under Grace?* let the light search thee, and it will aske thee, how camest thou to be under Grace? Is not the law for cleansing; When wast thou cleansed? or where dost thou think to be cleansed? Doth not Christ Jesus say, that he is come to fulfill the Law, and that one jot nor tittle[7] shall pass unfulfilled, and wilt thou speak of his words, and not believe him? Yea, thou shalt know, that for that very end is there a measure of Christ given unto thee; that if thou deny thy selfe, and yeeld obedience to his will, thou shalt witnesse the whole Law fulfilled in thee,[8] but it is through judgement, and through burning, for through judgement is Zion redeemed: but *hearken a little, and consider, hear and thy soule shall live.* If thou be willing to take up the Crosse of Christ, and despise the shame, thou shalt witnesse pure peace of conscience: and though it may seem hard to the world, yet there is living refreshments: Yea, glorious is the worke of redemption, but none can see it but those that come through it: And now the way of eternall life is laid before thee, if thou slight it, it shall lye at thy doore: and therefore take heed what thou dost; for when the booke of conscience is opened, thou shalt witnesse thou hast been warned in thy life-time.

Martha Simmonds

NOTES
  1. Luke, 19.41, 'And when he was come near he beheld the city and wept over it.'
  2. Matt. 7.22, 'And many will say to me in that day, Lord, Lord, have we not prophesied in thy name.' Matt. 23, 'And then I will profess unto them, I know you know.'
  3. Typological connection between the story of Genesis and Parable of the steward and talents (Matt. 25).
  4. Matt. 14.
  5. Job 5.5.
  6. Rom. 5.4.
  7. Matt. 5.8.
  8 Matt. 1.22.

51

Appendix Two

A LAMENTATION
For The lost Sheep of the House *of Israel*

Oh *England England* whom[1] art thou; groping in the darke and stumbling at noon day;[2] art thou grown so high[3] in thy fallen wisdome, and in the pride to a measure of God in thee? thou of thy fallen heart, that thou canst not stoop high professor, and thou wilde wanton one,[4] thou ranst so fast over the field to finde the Pearle;[5] there is a Royall Diadem[6] hid in thy uncleane heart, which never consented to the evill thereof; Oh that thou wouldst barken to it that thy inward eye might be opened, then wouldst thou see the beauty of it; surely if thou didst but see thy soule in death, and a measure of the light and life of Jesus there, checking, calling; and knocking,[7] to have thee turne in thy minde to it, that thou mayest be purged and cleansed,[8] and that it may shine forth and bring up thy soule out of the horrible pit;[9] then wouldst thou begin to know indeed what pure redemption is: And here mayest thou come to see that faith which purifies the heart, which is the reall substance of things hoped for, and this would be of more value to thee than thousands of Gold and Silver: Oh vaine and foo[2]lish man and woman that maketh not God thy trust, but trusts in the arme of flesh, and in the multitude of thy conceivings; how soone art thou affrighted and palenesse strikes thee in the face, and the least stirring or rushing in the creation[10] makes thy knees smite together and thy countenance fall, and this is because thou art in *Caines*[11] condition, and hast no habitation in God; and though thou mayest offer a Sacrifice, and pray, and cry, and confesse thy sinnes,[12] and cover the Alter with teares, and give thy body to be burnt, it in that nature it is not acceped. But this I shall say to thee, Oh that thou couldst but hear; if thou wouldst but submit thy neck to the yoak[13] of Christ, the measure of him in thee, that thou mayest see him to work in thee and thy own workes laid aside, thou wouldst finde more peace and satisfaction both to soule and body; and then shouldst thou see him who is the Rock of ages to be thy Rock, and strong defence, and then shouldst thou see a war[14] begin contrary to thy will and him that brings into the war and carries through, and then there would be nothing to doe on thy part but to stand still and keep thy minde in, girt up to him that works, and then thou wilt come to see what it is to follow the Lamb[15] through the tribulation; but if thou wilt not improve thy measure of Light, but wilt run on in thy headstrong rebellion against that little secret love that checks thee in private, and shewes thee thy heart when none else can, and if thou slight this day of small things, then will this precious Pearl, the measure of Light, be taken from thee and given to him that is more worthy; and the gnawing worme[16] will enter into thee, which will never die, but will torment thee to all eternity, and then wilt thou be shut up in darknesse and unbeliefe; where thou mayest say to thy soule, *take thy thine ease, eate drink and be merry, for tomorrow shall be as this day*,[17] and much more; but thou foole in this night, of thy darknesse, shall thy soule be taken from thee, and then what will thy small time of pleasures doe thee [3] good? will they not ad to thy torment? therefore I counsell thee to prise thy time, and be still and staid and seek diligently for that messenger, who is one of a thousand,[18] who brings the glad tidings,[19] who is the true teacher that cannot be removed into a corner, the corner stone,[20] who if thou abide will break thy heart to peeces, and will convince thee of thy sinne, and of thy right-eousnesse, and bring his pure Judgements upon it, that his right-eousnesse may appear.

And now to you high Priests of this Nation; and teachers of all sorts of opinions, who have been groping and hunting in your wisdome to finde out that precious Pearle to defile in your filthy nature; but you have not yet found it, nor cannot finde the doore to enter into the kingdome, nor get your starved hearers a little bread of assurance of eternal life; only this you can do to ad to your condemnation, gather up the Saints conditions of sufferings and patience, who were persecuted by the same proud high flowne nature that you are in, and you add your meanings to them, and so bring the curses that are written in that book[21] upon your heads, it is time for you now, seeing you cannot finde a way, to give over stealing from your neighbour, and be content with that you have, and let the people alone to the measure of God in them, that that may guide them into the way that they may finde bread for their soules; and seeing you will not enter your selves, do not shut the kingdome against them, in laying stumbling blocks[22] before them, and raising up false accusations against the Light and those that walk in it,[23] and casting a lie into the mouths of the ignorant prople, in saying the letter is the word, when the letter declares that the word was in the beginning, by which word the world was made, which word all the Saints and servants of God was ever guided by; which word enquired of your father *Caine* for *Abels* blood, which translated *Enoch*,[24] which word called *Abraham*[25] out of his own country to follow the Lord in a strange land, who was no vagrant person, which word [4] called *Moses* from the glory of *Pharoahs* house,[26] which word in due time was made manifest in flesh, who wandered up and down in dens and caves of the earth, who had no certaine abiding place, and yet he was no vagabond, whom your generation crucified, who is risen againe, and hath taken upon him the seed of *Abraham*, who is now appeared in this day of his power, to gather up his elect into himselfe, and to rip of all your deceitfull covering; and lay you open to the flame of the Heathen; and this is the word that we witnesse to lead and guide and command us whose mindes are staid in it; and this word moves us into your Idols temple and to other private meetings, to discover your Image of mixture of several opinions; untill you stop our mouths, and hale us forth, and deliver us up to your Rulers, who second you in your persecution, who imprison us, and scourge, and stock, and stone,[27] and despitefully use, and by the power of this word are we brought through these tribulations, and have joy in the midst of them, and when we are reviled we revile not againe taking patiently all that you have power in your wills to inflict upon us, and we are made able to desire the Lord not to lay these things to your charge, and that he would open your eyes that you might see what you are a doing, and then you would soon cease your rage and finde enough to doe within in your own hearts; and by this word we see the Scriptures were given forth from this word, and as we come into these severall conditions and measures that the Saints were in that spake forth the Declaration, we can set to our seale that the Scriptures are true, and they are ours, that live in the life, and not yours who despise the life, and feed your selves with words, and gather up to your selves great riches, in that nature, you eat greed-ily of the tree of knowledge, and now if you could but get to eate

54

of the tree of life[28] you would soon be above God; but that you cannot doe, for there stands a flaming sword that turns every way to keep you out,[29] so that all that comes there comes through it and leaves all [5] the first wisdome behinde; and therefore if any of you be found worthy to come down to the measure of Christ and submit your necks to his yoad it will be good for you, but not many rich nor many wise doe come to know these things; and we have the Promise of this word, that he will be with us unto the end of the world, and we know that his Promise is yea and amen.[30]

And now all people that hath sobriety, and love to your souls, come out from among the Idoll dumb Shepheards that feed themselves, but not you, and if you put not into their mouths they will soon shew violence[31] to you: come out from among them and be no longer partaker of their uncleannesse, for they are broken cisterns that can no longer hold water; and come into the fountaine[32] that runs forth freely, the streams whereof would refresh your hungry fainting soules: in my fathers house there is bread enough; Oh why will you perish for hunger? Minde the light the measure of Christ in you, that with it you may see where you are, that you may see his eternal love, how he alls and invites you into the Kingdome, that he may take off your filthy garments, and that he may cloath you with the garment of righteousnesse,[33] and marry you into himself; and now the day of his mighty power is appeared, and the fountaine of life set open to wash and cleanse you from your sinnes, and baptize you into his death and sufferings: Oh be not stubborn and stiffe-necked against him, for we that doe follow him finde his path[e]s pleasant pure and sweet,[34] and the further we follow him in the straight gate and narrow way, we see that his love is past finding out: And now in the tendernesse of my heart longing for your soules good am I made open to you, having had a [H]abitation in this City of *London* sometime; for seven years together I wandered up and down the streets enquiring of those that had the Image of honestie in their countenance, where I might finde an honest Minister, for I saw my soul in death, and that I was in the first nature, and wandring from one Idolls temple to another, and from one private [6] meeting to another, I heard a sound of words amongst them but no substance I could finde, and the more I sought after them the more trouble came on me, and finding none sensible of my condition, I kept it in, and kept all close within me; and about the end of seven years hunting, and finding no rest, the

Lord opened a little glimmerings of light to me, and quieted my spirit; and then for about seven years more he kept me still from running after men, and all this time I durst not meddle with any thing of God, nor scarce take his name in my mouth, because I knew him not, it living wilde and wanton not knowing a crosse to my will I spent this time; it something I found breathing in me groaning for deliverance,[35] crying out, oh when shall I see the day of thy appearance; about the end of the last seven years the Lord opened my eyes to see a measure of himselfe in me, and which when I saw I waited diligently in it, and being faithful to it I found this Light more and more increase, which brought me into a day of trouble, and through it, and through a warfare and to the end of it, and now hath given me a resting place with him; *and this is by beloved and this is my friend O daughters of Jerusalem*: And now all that have a desire to come this way must lay down your Crowns at the feet of Jesus, for now a profession of words will no longer cover, for the Lord is come to look for fruit, all types and shaddowes is flying away; and he that will come in may inherit substance and he that will not shall be left naked.

FINIS

NOTES
1. The Thomason tract has a hand written amendment to read 'where' which the 1656 text reads.
2. Deut. 28.29. John, 11.9-10.
3. Ps. 18.27, Is. 14.10.
4. 1 Tim. 5, 11. Jas. 5, 5.
5. Matt. 13.45.
6. Is. 62.3.
7. Rev. 3.20.
8. Ps. 51.7.
9. Ps. 40.2.
10. Rom. 8.22.
11. Gen. 4.11, 12, 15.
12. Reference to the rituals of Catholicism.
13. Matt. 1.29.
14. 'War' was often used by Quaker writers as a reference to inner conflict. War imagery is common in Quaker writings as many of them had served in Cromwell's army and saw the civil wars in a prophetic context.

15. Another common Quaker term for the contemporary religious turmoil. 'War of the Lamb,' 'lamb's tribulation,' were commonly used by Nayler, Fox and others.
16. Jon. 4.7.
17. 1 Cor. 15.32.
18. The number 'one thousand' appears throughout the Old and New Testaments to symbolise a limitless figure.
19. Luke 2.10, 11.
20. Job. 38.6. Eph. 2.20.
21. Rev. 22.29, 20.
22. Ezek. 3.30., 1 Cor. 1.23.
23. The persecutions suffered by the Quakers.
24. Gen. 1.17. Enoch was the child of Cain's wife.
25. Gen. 12.1.
26. Ex. 3.3, 4.
27. Persecutions suffered by the Quakers.
28. An oblique reference to the fall, Gen. 3.3.
29. According to the Book of Genesis, Lucifer was banished from heaven by the Archangel Michael with a flaming sword for attempting to be above God.
30. Rev. 20.21.
31. Quakers disputed the clergy's right to the collection of tithes.
32. Rev. 27.17-18.
33. Rev. 3.3.
34. Ps. 23.
35. Rom. 8.23.

Appendix Three

O ENGLAND: THY TIME IS COME

**(c.1657 by James Nayler, Martha Simmons,
Hannah Stranger and William Tomlinson)**

O England; thy time is come, God hath not taken
thee until thou be ful; yea, the fulness of thy time is
come; with speed prepare to meet the Lord in
Judgement, lest thou be cut off; wo unto thee if he
turn from thee before thou be refined. Remember,
was not the Jewes cut off that thou might be grafted
in? Remember and take heed

J.N

Ye men of Galilee, why stand yee gazing up into heaven?
This same Jesus which is taken up from you into heaven
shall so come in like manner as ye have seen him go into
heaven. Acts 1.11

This glorious Reign of Christ is come;
Ho! everyone behold the Sonne:
This is the beautiful Morning-Star
Who sends his Messengers through the air
And calls up all to Judgement; O hast and come away
You Virgins that are ready! this is the Marriage-Day.

You foolish Virgins,[1] how have you been sleeping away your
precious time? had it not been better you had watcht and prayed?
O foolish, foolish Children, will you sell your birthright for a
moments pleasure, and a little ease? But what more can be said to
you; I see the Spirit is grieved with you, and the Spirit is weary
with striving with you: O that I could weep tears of blood for the

slackness of the desires of the people concerning their eternal salvation! Is your souls of no more value then to make a sport of time? O England! thou hast not wanted for Warnings; my soul stands witness in the presence of the lord against thee, that in thy Cities, Towns, and Market-Streets, I have past with bitter cryes and streams of tears, for a most two [2] yeers time, warning you of this day that is coming upon you as a Snare, with this Lamentation, O people of England repent! O that thou wouldest consider the time of thy visitation! O that thou wouldest prise thy time before the dore of Mercy is shut! Now the Light is risen, how art thou found slaying the Lamb of God? in thee is found slain the blood of the Innocent; O England! the blood of the Innocent cries loud in the ears of the Lord God of Power; O that thou wouldest condsider and repent, and prise thy time before thou be consumed and made a common deluge for ever! Thou art fat and full,[2] thou art fitted for slaughter, and great and terrible will thy day of calamity be; the Sword of the Lord[3] is drawn against thee, and will be sheathed in thy bowels. O repent! repent, and let the destruction of *Sodom*[4] be a warning to thee O England! fitted for slaughter; thou art light and vain, thou kicks against the Lord, thou lifts up thy heel against him; O England, the time is come that nothing will satisfie but blood; yea, yea the time is come that nothing will satisfie but blood: Thou art making thy self drunken with the blood of the Innocent; he will be avenged of thee; till blood come up to the Horses bridle;[5] hou art making thy self drunken with the blood of the innocent, and now he will give thee blood to drink, for thou art worthy; for he will be avenged of thee till he is satisfied with thy blood: Come down ye high and lofty ones and lie in the dust, and repent in sack-cloath, and lie low before the Lord and come and see if by any means there may be a place for repentance found.

This mournful cry began at *London*, so to *Colchester*, and through the Nation: Ah Lord! what shall I yet say for them? or how shall I enter into a Treaty for them? Behold, they have slighted thy tenders of Grace, and they wipe their mouths, and take their fills of mirth; and they wipe their mouths, and cry, *Tush, the Lord is gone far off;* they cry *Miracles are ceast, and there is no Revelation; tush the Lord seeth not*: When thy servants have shewed them thy minde, they have said, *Let him do his worst.* O Lord arise in thy zeal, and shew thy power, for they blaspheme thy Name conti[3]nually; how they have slighted thy love, now thou hast visited the earth with thy pure voice? how cruelly have they beaten thy Prophets, and now thy Son is come they conspire to kill him?

Generation of unbelievers! now is not the Scripture fulfilled that faith, *When the Son of Man come: shall he finde faith upon the earth?* Is it not seen that you love the world too well? you look for the reign of Christ, I know you do, for there is that in your consciences which sheweth you that your soul is in death, and waits for redemption; but how have you slighted the Messenger of reconciliation, that hath told you in secret that you should come away and leave your vanities, it had been well if you had minded the check and re-proof, if you had done so, your hearts had been purified, then now you had been ready to meet him; when he fulfilled all Righteousness, and ascended unto his Father, he gave down his spirit among you, which hath visited your Fathers and you unto this day, which was to minister unto you, untill his second coming:[6] But how hath your ears been stopt against it, did it he ever appear in such an age before? But now the Heavens is loaded with a Blessing, and there is not room in the earth to receive it, make room, make room, enlarge your hearts, for it is there that he will reign I see, and as your hearts is enlarged, you will come down as *Zicheus*[7] did, for he is made a little lower than the Angels, that so he may raise up the innocent Seed which lies scattered in your dark hearts: As far as you are obedient to the spirit that preaches to your souls in prison, so far you make room for his reigne, so far you become Members of the body, for now he hath prepared for you a Leader and a Captain; doth not your eyes see the Lord hath prepared him a body fitted for sufferings in patience, which he hath crown'd with love and meekness; so that the more you torture him, the more he loves, yet you cannot see; but to you that live in hope my heart is enlarged, yet to see the redemption of *Zion,* and to enjoy he glorious Reign of Christ; the Lord give you the desire of your souls, for now is your time to receive; Wherefore I beseech you sit you under your own vine,[8] feed in peace, go [4] not forth after them that crye, Lo here, and Lo there, for they are false Watch-men, they will smite you, and bereave you of your fresh springs which you should enjoy in the spirit; but watch low and still in you mindes, and with that which is just, judge that which is unjust; and when your wills would have Liberty, let it be crost with the Light; then you will see that in your obedience you will have peace, and the peace that your obedience will bring, will so knit your hearts to the Lord, that nothing will be too hard for you; then comes your hearts to be opened to receive the Blessing, and your mindes stedfast in Communion with the Lord; He will visit you with his fresh springs, and cause the seed to grow; and as it grows up to God, it brings the Son down to you, who is given into the world to redeem your souls from the power of sin and death, and so as he purifies you with judgement, so your Temples[9] will be fitted for Christ to rule and reign in you, and then comes his will to be done in the earth as it is in Heaven; and as your hearts, mindes and affections incline to the Lord, you will see faith encrease, and by patient waiting in hope, you will see the Hills levelled, and the mountains laid low[10] of sin and corruption; and when the Lord hath pluckt your feet out of the Snare, and set you upon a plain, then will you run the way of his commandments with great delight; and this is the State of Virginity. Oh you noble hearts! It is you that are fit to entertaine Christ in his reign, for in your obedience the precious springs of Life doth open in you, and pure consolation you feele, Songs of Joy and Triumph, and the Father, Son and Spirit meets in you; then hath the soul Liberty from the devouring Enemy; as the pure Spirit gets Victory over the evil Spirit, so the Spirit of Christ comes to reign in your mortal bodies, then comes the flowers of Grace as the morning-due which bathes your souls in the blood of the Lamb, and wars the tender Plant in you. This is a wise Virgin[11] that is ready to meet the Bridegroom in the his day; I counsel you that have oyle to trim your Lamps; and prepare to meet the Lamb, for now it is full time, for he that was to come, is come, and his time is short, and then no more time, make [5] haste away you Virgins of the daie, for time is short, for now is the time of sealing come, he that is filthie, let him be filthie still; and he that is holie must be received into the bodie. Now blessed are you that are found ready; for now we see there hath been terrible wars betwixt *Michael*[12] and the Dragon[13] to make room for the Babe;[14] not one step but thorow blood that we can get entertainment amongst you; but now I see the foundation is firmly & deeply laid through sufferings, and now set your Battel never so strong, it will grow more firm; but blessed be the peace-makers, for they are fit to have the Mansion in my Fathers Kingdom.[15] Why should it seem a strange thing to you to see Christ reigne in his Saints and sit and prepare the Vessels, and make our bodies fit for himself to dwell in, seeing our hearts are ready to bow to his Will? And is it not more for his glory, though it be a greater

61

cross to your wills, to purifie these bodies, and pour out the dregs thereof, then to bring down that body which was crucified at Jerusalem, seeing all are in his power and one Spirit rules in both; by much tribulation, anguish of Spirit, and sufferings of the flesh, hath he now fitted a bodie for himself, who hath conquered death and hell; so perfect is he that he can lay down his life for his enemies,[16] not opening his mouth to defend himself, this Vessel is as precious to me as that which was tortured at Jerusalem,[17] seeing the Father hath prepared them both, and the same Graces springs from both according to its time of working, which now is finisht in sufferings. Shall I not follow thee unto death, O my beloved? yes, seeing thou art revealed in me by my Father to be the Son of Peace.

Now what though he was brought up with you? Despite him not as your fathers did; but the Scriptures must be fulfilled, *A Prophet is not without honor but in his own Country;* surely if you knew the bowels of love that flows to you; you would be more meek, what shall we do to declare our love? the Lord knows we love all men, from the Magistrate to the meanest, and delight to live in love and peace with all men; and if any do lord it over you, and judge you in their Wills, they must be judged. Now I beseech you, is not this the man[6]ner of the reign of Christ, to purifie the bodies of his Saints to make them Temples for himself, and quicken them by his Spirit? and he that leads the way is the Captain, King, or Prophet, which in all ages the people loved and honoured; Would you were worthy to receive the salvation of his love and peace, which the showers of his rain hath brought, his Reign is glorious. Now hearts are knit together in unity each to other, and Praises springs up freely up to the Father of all, and here is none shut out who is real hearted: Whether ever we see your faces outwardly, yet I am sure if you love the Lord, and be obedient to him, we shall meet in Spirit, and that Spirit will reveal to you that Innocency must be King. Therefore friends all, use the World as if you used it Not; for the time is very short, and every one shall be taken where is; he that is filthy, shall be filthy still; and he that is holy, shall be holy still; for no place of Repentance shall be left; and many shall say, Lord, we preached in thy Name, and in thy Name we have cast out Devils, and done many wonderful things, but he shall say unto them, Depart ye Workers of Iniquity, I know you not; and they shall flie into the Dens and Caves of the earth,[18,19] and shall call to the Mountains and Rocks to fall on them, and cover them from the glory of his presence. Watch, Watch, the time hasteth exceedingly, when time shall be no more, for the Gate shall be shut, and no place left for Repentance.

Martha Simmonds.

There's none can reigne with Christ but he
That is a Virgin pure in innocency.
No evil thoughts nor worc's must be,
For that will stain Virginity.

how excellent is thy waies thou God of Mercy and Truth! Surely they that go out of thy pathes are not worthy to walk therein; they that forget thy love, have not found the sweetness of it; why should it be that any that have known thy Word should cast it behinde their backs. But let my soul cleave to thy Statutes, & let obedience be my life continualie; so shall I be acquainted with thy will, O Lord, thou knowest I love thy counsel, and in it my heart pondereth;[20] and if thou wilt open thy bosom, and let me come nearer to thee, that is all I desire; but let me remember thy former mercies for they are life, how hast thou led me through the Desarts, and refreshed me with thy Christal Streams & gave me Manna for food?[21] How gentlie didst thou guide me when all comforts failed me, and removed the mountains out of my way, and hath set me upon a plane, that I run the way of thy Commandments with great delight? Why hath thy Rod been so light upon me, seeing my sins have been multiplied? How have I scaped the Rod of thine anger? nay, thou didst put a Rod into my hand, to smite the backslider and hard-hearted : O Lord, thou knowest it was thy will, I did not resist thee. Oh that they might know it, the rod, and who it was that did appoint it! and now thou hast taken it out of my-hand, and bowed me to thy will, and hath opened a door of Mercie to all sorts of people; Oh let thy Mercie shower down abundantlie, and fill the earth with thy Blessing; that thy Works may praise thee, for now praises [9] are readie for thee, and many hearts panteth after thee, that have long lain amongst the pots; all the upright love thee, for they have been as a chased Roe upon the Mountains,[22] which have wanted a Shepherd, wherefore arise O Lord, and visit the Nations with thy appearance, that they may know thy salvation.

Martha Simmonds.

Oh my beloved! Where hast thou been hidden? clefts of the Rocks? And I could by no means finde thee, though I have sought thee day & night with a mournful and bleeding heart?[23] But when I was still and patient, then thou didst appear to me with pure consolation, and then we did sup together;[24] but then thou wouldest withdraw again, and then my soul would mourn, for I saw thy presence was my life and preservation. Thou didst command me forth into thy Work, to invite those in which knew thee not, and I was obedient to thee; when I returned and gave thee an account,[25] thou didst accept my service, though men denied it, and thou gavest into my bosom a double Blessing. Oh! how thou hast drawn me unto thee, & inclin'd my heart to thy will; how hast thou indeared my soul within thy bosom? Thou hast tried me, and in thy trial thou hast found me steadfast; it all that I desired of thee was, and is, That thou wouldest wholly take me into the Counsel: I ever loved thy Reproof, and dreaded thy Anger; for I finde correction is as balm to me, and I have not murmured at them. Oh pure, eternal, perfect Lord God! when I came neer to know thee, it was life for evermore, for thy presence overcame me; but how have I been tossed to and fro in this dark world? Surely thou hadst a purpose to make use of me in thy will and time; for the devil hath set very sore against me; for before ever I saw the Light of the Sun, or received a natural birth in this visible World, I was rejected of men, for my [10] Parents denied me a birth; and as concerning self, it had been good I had not been born; for I have not had pleasure in this world, but have stood as one alone; and since I knew the way to thee, I have exceedingly hasted out of it; and before I knew the way; I sought for the way to all that pretended to direct the way; but they had stoln thy words, & had not thy life so they wearied me, and profited me not; but now thou hast revealed thy son in me Oh! How am I overcome with thy presence? and now I shall live with thee for ever.

MS.

NOTES

1. Matt. 25.3-13.
2. Ezek. 39.14.
3. The sword in scripture is often used as a symbol for war. Gen. 27.40.
4. The city of Sodom was destroyed by God for its sinfulness. Gen. 13.10.
5. Rev. 14.20.

6. Jn. 16, 8-13.
7. Luke 19.5.
8. 1 Kings 4.25.
9. Acts 6.19.
10. Jer. 4.24.
11. Matt. 25.3-15.
12. Dan. 10.13.
13. Reference to the Fall and Satan.
14. Christ.
15. John 14.2.
16. 3 John 4.
17. Christ, but also an elliptical reference to Nayler.
18. See *A Lamentation*, 1.99.
19. Ps. 23.
20. Ps. 119.
21. Ex. 35, Rev. 2.17.
22. 1 Chron. 12.8.
23. S.of.S. 6.2,3.
24. *Ibid.* 5.1.
25. See *When the Lord Jesus*, 1.13.

Appendix Four

LETTER FROM MARTHA SIMMONS TO WILLIAM DEWSBURY

The Letter thus.

Oh let me for evermore be tried by the hands of Jesus. But should it enter into the heart of my Lord, concerning his Servant of being guilty in this matter; would my life could go forever for Israell, for it is not I that troubleth it, neither am I guilty in this matter: Oh that I were before thee a little, that thou mayest try mee, for I Know thou canst discerne simplicity. But the time is not yet come, though not far off. But keep thy Temple clear, where the beauty of holiness is, and let no thought nor jealousie enter, to cause thee to stumble innocency, for I see the Lord is arising as one coming up from the wine presse of his Fathers wrath, and he catcheth at the refuge of lies and cleaves all before him, like a refiners fire, then shall all behold innocencie.

In her Examination she saies she cal[l]s him Lord, and that she ought to worship him so that he is that Jesus by whose hand she would be tied. As in the beginning of the Letter.

The Examination of MARTHA SYMONDS the wife of THOMAS SYMONDS of London, Stationer

Question *Why did you sing before James Nayler holy, holy, &c. When he rode into* Bristoll, *and led his horse!* Answer I know not James Nayler. *Q. Do you know there was such a one? A.* He was but now is past to a more pure estate, and the power of the

Martha Simonds Examination. The image is born up.

66

Lord carried me to sing and lead his horse. Q. Hannah Stranger *in her Letter calls him* the fairest of ten thousand the hope of Israeli, the only begotten Son of God: *Is* James Nailer *so?* A. For *James Nailer* he is buried in Mee, and have promised to come the second time. Q. *Do you believe it was well to call and stile him so as in the Letter? A.* I cannot judge them. Q. *Why did you lead his horse and fall on your knees before him? A.* In obedience to the power on high. Q. *Why did you fall down and worship him? A.* I ought to do it. Q. *Is* James *Nayler the everlasting Son of Righteousnesse? A.* He is the Son of Righteousnesse; and the new man wrought up in him, is the everlasting Son of Righteousnesse. And when the new life shall be borne in *James Nailer,* then he will be *Jesus.* But for the fulnes of it he doth not know its yet born up, *you say* James Nailer *is buried?* Q. *What do you call him? A.* I call him Lord. Q. *Why Lord? A.* He is Lord of Righteousnesse and prince of peace. Q. *Why King of Israell: In what sence? A.* He is anointed King of Israill. Q. *By Whom? A.* By[]a prophet. Q. *By what prophet? A.* Let that alone, I will not answ[e]r it. Being asked whether she spread her cloathes: &c. She acknowledged that she did. Quest. *Doth that Spirit of Jesus in Nailer enable him to be a Jesus to another? A.* I say there is a seed borne in him which I shall honour above all men. Q. *Your husband calls him King of Israell; Is he so? A.* Then you have a double Testimony.

So that he is worshipped by Them. As after.

67

Burrough, Francis Howgill and George Whitehead occur. By 1657 Simmonds was printing more than Calvert, and his output included most of Fox's work and Burrough's polemics. The following year saw more than fifty items issued from Thomas Simmonds' press, including pamphlets by most of the leading Friends. At this time Simmonds was forced, like Calvert before him, to entrust to others some of his printing, and thus we find George Rofe's *Revelation of God* printed on his behalf by Roger Norton, junior. In 1659 Simmonds' total production for Friends was nearly a hundred and twenty items. This uneasy period evoked many outbursts from Edward Burrough, and a dozen of these were issued by Simmonds, but perhaps his outstanding publication of the year was Nayler's prison-writing, *What the Possession of the Living Faith is, and the Fruits thereof.* In the following year he printed in folio Fox's omnibus reply to hostile critics: *The Great Mistery of the Great Whore unfolded.* From the Restoration Simmonds' output fell away to sixty-nine in 1660, twenty in 1661 and one in 1662. During these years he continued to publish exhortations to those in authority, and accounts of sufferings. His final recorded imprint is on William Bayly's Life of Enoch again Revived (1662).

DICTIONARY OF PRINTERS AND BOOKSELLERS: 1641 to 1667 BY HENRY R. PLOMER

SIMMONS (THOMAS), bookseller in London; Bull and Mouth near Aldersgate, 1656-62. Publisher of Quaker books.

CALVERT (GILES), bookseller in London; Black-Spread-Eagle, St. Paul's Churchyard, 1639-64. Son of George Calvert, of Meere, in the county of Somerset, 'clerk,' and brother of George Calvert, *q.v.* He was first apprenticed to William Lugger, bookseller, for nine years from June 30th, 1628, but for some reason not stated his indentures were cancelled, and he took out fresh indentures on June 11th, 1631, for the remainder of his term, seven years, with Joseph Hunscott. [Stationers' Register of Apprenticeships.] He took up his freedom on January 25th, 1639. [Arber, iii.688.] He is chiefly noted as the publisher of the early Quaker literature, but so far as is at present known he was not openly of that society. On Cromwell's accession to power Giles Calvert, with Henry Hills and Thomas Brewster, was appointed official 'printer' to the Council of State. This appointment shows that he was in favour with the Government, and explains how it was that he was able to publish Quaker books without restraint. On only one occasion, in 1656, does he appear to have been questioned, but nothing serious seems to have followed. [*State Papers*, 1656, p.308.] In 1661 he was arrested and thrown into prison for publishing a pamphlet entitled *The Phoenix of the Solemn League and Covenant*, but he was released after a few weeks' confinement. He is believed to have died about April, 1664, and was succeeded in his business by his widow, Elizabeth Calvert.

CHAPMAN (LIVEWELL), bookseller in London, (1) Crown in Pope's Head Alley, 1651-61; (2) In Exchange Alley in Cornhill, 1665. Son of Edward Chapman, of London, scrivener. Apprenticed to Benjamin Allen November 6th, 1643, for seven years. Married, between 1650 and 1653, the widow of Benjamen Allen. [Stat. Reg., Liber E, f.249.] In 1655 Chapman was apprehended for printing seditious pamphlets, and amongst the Thurloe State Papers [vol. 4, p.379] is an interesting letter from Col. Barkstead, in which he says that Chapman 'is the owner or at least a sharer in the private press, that hath and doth soe much mischiefe ....' He is said to have been the compiler of a notorious tract entitled *The Phoenix of the Solemn League and Covenant* in 1661, for the publication of which Thomas Brewster, Giles Calvert and others were punished. Amongst his other publications may be noticed an edition of Sir John Harrington's *Oceana*, published in 1655.

EPILOGUE

KATE PETERS, in her 2005 publication: *Print Culture and the Early Quakers* describes (page 129) Margaret Fell and Martha Simmons as the 'most prolific of the [early Quaker] women authors', with Margaret Fell as the 'chief co-ordinator' of the rapidly expanding movement and with Martha Simmons as 'a charismatic leader ... in London'.

Martha Simmons was near the centre of Quakerism from her youth, being the sister of Giles Calvert and the wife of Thomas Simmonds (from 1655), who in London were the first two publishers of Quaker books and tracts. After her early Anglican background she had been convinced of the Quaker message in 1654, at the age of thirty, and between 1656 and 1658 she wrote three printed tracts.

This present book has reproduced the complete text of these, together with the author's detailed analysis of them, and thus enables present-day readers to re-assess for themselves Martha's contribution to early Quaker history, especially in the context of her leading of James Nayler's horse (not donkey) in his controversial and tragic entry into Bristol (not at Easter) but on Friday 24th October in 1656. (Attention should also be drawn to page 20 where the author quotes contemporary evidence that Nayler with his group had recently also made 'Jesus entries' into both Wells and Glastonbury).

Upon apprehension by the Bristol magistrates, James was foolishly carrying an adulatory letter written by two others in the group: Hannah and John Stranger: describing James as 'the only begotten Son of God' and declaring 'Thy name is no more to be called James but Jesus'.

No Bristol-based Quakers are named in the 1656 Nayler trials (just the seven named itinerants), out of perhaps one thousand Quaker activists then resident in Bristol: certainly George Bishop, a leading Bristol Quaker, disapproved. All the small itinerant group were thrown into prison and sharply questioned. Nayler was first tried in Bristol and convicted of blasphemy for emulating the entry of Jesus into Jerusalem. He was then sent to London and tried by a Committee of the House of Commons (no less) for several weeks. A death penalty against Nayler was only defeated by 96 votes to 82. These long-drawn-out and involved proceedings are closely examined by Professor William Bittle of Kent University, USA in his *James Nayler: Quaker Indicted by Parliament* (1986). Nayler was barbarically punished, close to the point of death, producing in him a holy spirit of forgiveness despite a ravaged body.

James Nayler's Bristol entry was only four years after Fox's great Firbank Fell year of 1652 and so before there was any form of organisation for the new religious sect. If God spoke into the heart of anyone, there was urgent compulsion immediately to follow that bidding, whether God's message was to leave wife and Yorkshire farm (as with Nayler); to visit the Sultan of Turkey (without the knowledge of the language); to walk semi-naked through a 'wicked' town in sackcloth and ashes (as with Samuel Eccles and a few others including Martha herself); or to persuade someone to ride into Bristol, accompanied by Hosannahs. Posterity might think that the way was therefore open to religious excess and proliferation of aims and beliefs.

In hindsight it now seems evident that this controversial Bristol entry caused a needed reaction by George Fox, Margaret Fell and the other leaders of the then largely rule-less early Quaker Movement, namely that individuals and small groups needed to bring their deep spiritual leadings for endorsement by the wider Quaker community, *before* implementing what they deeply believed God was calling them to do.

Encouragement was increasingly given for the setting up of Monthly Meetings in each small geographic area, open for all Quakers wishing to attend, additional to the presence of named representatives from the individual Meetings for Worship in the area.

It was in November 1656 (one month after Nayler's entry into Bristol) that Balby General Meeting (in south Yorkshire) issued a long series of practical words of advice. Nothing there was directly minuted about James Nayler's alleged blasphemy – but the acceptance of the Balby advices indicated that the worshipping group had become ready to receive corporate guidance.

Wisely this Balby Minute of November 1656 was given in a spirit of gentle advice.

> Dearly beloved friends, these things we do not lay upon you as a rule or form to walk by, but that all with the measure of light which is pure and holy may be guided, and so in the light walking and abiding these may be fulfilled in the Spirit, – not from the letter, for the letter killeth, but the Spirit giveth life.
>
> (Braithwaite's *Beginnings of Quakerism*, p.311)

Thereupon and so continuing to this present day, it is recommended Quaker procedure that whenever a Quaker 'feels a leading or calling from God' or 'feels a strong religious personal concern', then their recommended first step is to put their leading/calling/religious concern before their local Meeting in order to seek the blessing, good wishes and tacit support of their worshipping community.

For these reasons, I believe that present-day Quakers may reflectively say: 'Thank you James: Thank you Martha'.

Bill Sessions
Sessions Book Trust
2008

BIBLIOGRAPHY

Primary Sources

(Books marked by an asterisk are published by Martha Simmons' family)

AUDLAND, John, *The Innocent delivered out of the Snare*, London, 1655.

BATHURST, Elizabeth, *Truth's Vindication, Or, A Gentle Stoke to wipe off the Foul Aspertions, false Accusations, and Misrepresent-ations, cast upon the People of God call'd Quakers*, London, 1695. (Published posthumously).

BESSE, Joseph, *A Collection of the Sufferings of the People called Quakers for the Testimony of a Good Conscience, from 1650-1689, Taken from Original Records and other Authentick Documents by Joseph Besse*, 2 vols., London, 1753. (Also: a series of ten Regional Volumes with new Indexes of People and of Places (from 1998-2008, Sessions of York).

BLACKBOROW, Sarah, *A Visit To The Spirit in Prison; And An Invitation to all people to come to Christ the light of the World, in whom is life, and doth enlighten every one that cometh into the World*, London, 1658.★

CARY, Mary, *A New and Exact Mappe*, London, 1651.★

DEACON, John, *An Exact History of the life of James Nayler*, London, 1657.

DEACON, John, *The Grand Imposter Examined: or, The Life Tryall and Examination of James Nayler, The Seduced and Seducing Quaker, with The Manner of his Riding into Bristol*, London, 1656.

ENGLISH BIBLE, King James (Authorised) Version.

EVANS, Arise, *The Declaration of Arise Evans*, London, 1654.★

FARNHAM, Edward, *James Nailors Recantation, Penned and directed by Himself to all the People of the Lord, Gathered and Scattered*, London, 1659.

FARMER, Ralph, *The Throne of Truth Exalted over the Powers of Darkness*, London, 1657.★

FARMER, Ralph, *Sathan Inthron'd in his Chair of Pestilence, or, Quakerism in its Exaltation*, London, 1666.

GARGILL, Anne, *A Warning to All the World,* London, 1656.*

GARGILL, Anne, *The Discovery of that Which is called the Popish Religion,* London, 1656.*

GRIGGE, William, *The Quakers Jesus,* London, 1658.

HYDE, Edward, *The Mystery of Christ in Us,* London, 1651.*

NAYLER, James, SIMMONS, Martha, STRANGER, Hannah, TOMLINSON, William, *O England thy Time is come,* London, c.1657.

PATTISON, B., *A Warning from the Lord to the Teachers and Peoples of Plimouth with a few Queries,* London, 1656.*

RICH, Robert and TOMLINSON, William, *A True Narrative of the Late Examination, Tryall and Sufferings of James Nayler,* London, 1657.

SIMMONS, Martha, *When the Lord Jesus,* London, printed for Giles Calvert, 1656.*

SIMMONS, Martha, *A Lamentation for the Lost Sheep of the House of Israel,* London, 1855.*

SIMMONS, Martha, *A Lamentation for the Lost Sheep of the House of Israel,* London, 1665, reprinted with *When the Lord Jesus came to Jerusalem,* London, 1656.*

WESTWOOD, Mary, *Papers sent to Parliament the twentieth day of the fifth Moneth, 1659. Being above seven thousand of the Names of the Handmaids and daughters of the Lord,* London, 1659.*

WHITE, Dorothy, *Upon the 22nd day of the 8th Month,* London, 1659.

WHITE, Dorothy, *A Diligent Search amongst Rulers, Priests, & People,* London, 1659.

Secondary Sources

ARMSTRONG, Karen, *The End of Silence: Women and the Priesthood,* London: Fourth Estate, 1993.

ASTON, Margaret, *Lollards and Reformers, Images and Literacy in Late Medieval Religion,* London: Hambleton Press, 1984.

AUGHTERSON, Kate, (ed.) *English Renaissance: an Anthology of Sources and Documents,* London: Routledge, 1998.

AUGHTERSON, Kate, *Renaissance Women: A Source Book,* London, New York: Routledge, 1985.

BARBOUR, Hugh, and ROBERTS, Arthur, O., *Early Quaker Writings, 1650-1700,* Grand Rapids: Eerdmans, 1973.

BAUMAN, Richard, *Let your words be few, Symbolism of speaking and silence among seventeenth-century Quakers,* Cambridge: Cambridge University Press, 1983.

BEILIN, Elaine V., *Redeeming Eve: Women Writers of the Renaissance*, Princeton, Oxford: Princeton University Press, 1987.

BELL, M., PARFITT, G., SHEPHERD, S., *A Biographical Dictionary of English Women Writers*, London: Harvester Wheatsheaf, 1990.

BELL, Maureen, 'Women in the English Book Trade,' *Leipziger Jahrbuch zur Buchgeschichte* 6, 1996, pp.13-45.

BELL, Maureen, 'Seditious Sisterhood: Women Publishers of Opposition at the Restoration' in Chedzgoy, *et al.*, pp.185-195.

BITTLE, Professor William G., *James Nayler: Quaker Indicted by Parliament*, Sessions of York in association with Friends United Press, Richmond, Indiana, 1986.

BOOY, David, (ed.) *Personal Disclosures: an Anthology of Self-Writings from the Seventeenth Century*, Aldershot: Ashgate, 2001.

BOWERS, Terence, 'Margery Kempe as Traveller,' *Studies in Philology*, 97, (1) 2000, pp.1-27.

BRAILSFORD, Mabel Richmond, *A Quaker from Cromwell's Army: James Nayler*, London: The Swarthmore Press, 1927.

BRAITHWAITE, William C., *The First Period of Quakerism*, London: MacMillan, 1919 (and from Sessions of York, 1970).

BRAITHWAITE, William C., *The Second Period of Quakerism*, London: MacMillan, 1919 (and from Sessions of York, 1979).

BRAYSHAW, A. Neave, *The Quakers their Story and Message*, Sessions, 1982, pp.133-137.

BRANT, Clare and PURKISS, Diane, *Women, Texts and Histories, 1575-1760*, London: Routledge, 1992.

BRINK, Andrew W., 'Paradise Lost's James Nayler's Fall,' *Journal of the Friends Historical Society, (J.F.H.S.)*, 53 (1) 1972.

CARROLL, K.L., 'Martha Simmonds, a Quaker Enigma,' *J.F.H.S*, (1) 1972, pp.31-52.

CARROLL, K.L., 'Sackcloth and Ashes and Other Signs and Wonders,' in *Journal of the Friends Historical Society*, 53, (1) 1975, pp.314-325.

CARROLL, K.L., 'Quaker Attitudes towards Signs and Wonders', *J.F.H.S.*, (2) 1977, pp.70-84.

CERASANO, S.P., and WYNNE-DAVIES, (eds) M., *Gloriana's Face, Women, Public and Private in the English Renaissance*, London: Harvester Wheatsheaf, 1992.

CHEDGZOY, Kate, 'Female Prophecy in the Seventeenth Century: the case of Anna Trapnel,' in Zunder, W. and Trill, S., *Writing in the English Renaissance*, London, 1996, pp.238- 253.

CHEDGZOY, Kate, HANSEN, Melanie and TRILL, Suzanne, (eds.) *Voicing Women: Gender and Sexuality in Early Modern Writing,* Edinburgh: Edinburgh University Press, 1998.

CHARTIER, Roger, 'Texts, Printing and Readings,' in HUNT, Lynne, (ed.) *The New Cultural History,* Berkeley: University of California Press, 1989.

CLARE, Janet, 'Transgressing Boundaries: Women's Writing in the Renaissance and Reformation,' *Renaissance Forum,* 1, (1), 1996. (http://www.hull.ac.uk/renforum).

CLARK, Alice, *Working Life of Women in the Seventeenth Century,* London: Cassell, 1968.

COHEN, Alfred, 'Prophecy and Madness: Women Visionaries during the Puritan Revolution,' *Journal of Psychohistory,* 11, 1984, pp.411-430.

COLLINSON, John, *The History and Antiquities of the County of Somerset, collected from authentick records, and an actual survey made by the late Mr. Edmumd Rack,* 3 vols., Bath: R. Crutwell, 1791.

COMO, David, 'Women, Prophecy and Authority in Early Stuart Puritanism,' *The Huntingdon Library Quarterly,* 61, 2000, pp.201-222.

CRAWFORD, Patricia, and GOWING, Laura, (eds.) *Women's Worlds in Seventeenth Century England: A Sourcebook,* London: Routledge,1999.

CRESSY, D., 'Levels of Literacy in England, 1530-1730,' *The Historical Journal,* 20, 1977, pp.1-23.

CRUDEN, Alexander, *Complete Concordance to the Old and New Testaments,* London: Lutterworth Press, 1951.

DAMROSCH, Leo, *The Sorrows of the Quaker Jesus, James Nayler and the Puritan Crackdown on the Free Spirit,* Cambridge (Massachusetts), London: Harvard University Press, 1996.

DAVIES, Adrian, *The Quakers in English Society,* Oxford: Oxford University Press, 2000.

DAVIES, C.S.L., *Peace, Print and Protestantism,* London: Fontana, 1995.

DICKENS, A.G., *The English Reformation,* London: Fontana, 1967.

DUGAN, Don-John, 'The London Book Trade in 1709,' *Publications of the Bibliographical Society of America,* 95 (1), 2001, pp.31-58.

EALES, Jacqueline, *Women in Early Modern England, 1500-1700,* London: Duckworth, 1998.

EDWARDS, George W., 'The Bull and Mouth Meeting House, its Site and Environs,' *The Friends Quarterly,* 6, 1955, pp.78-84.

FELL, Margaret, LETTERS, FUP Richmond, USA, 2003: Ed. Elsa F. Glines.

FELL, Margaret, *Mother of Quakerism*, Sessions, reprinted 1996 Isabel Ross.

FINDLAY, Sandra and HOBBY, Elaine, 'Seventeenth Century Women's Autobiography', *Proceedings of the Essex Conference on the Sociology of Literature, 1642: Literature and Power in the Seventeenth Century*, ed. Francis Barker *et.al.*, University of Essex, 1981, pp.11-36.

FOUGELKLOU, Emily, *James Nayler, the Rebel Saint, 1618-1660*, London: E. Benn, 1931.

FRASER, Antonia, *The Weaker Vessel*, New York: Vintage Books, 1984.

GARMAN, Mary *et al.*, *Hidden in Plain Sight, Quaker Women's Writings, 1650-1700*, Pennsylvania: Pendle Hill, 1996.

GRAHAM, Elspeth, (ed.) *Her Own Life, Writings by Seventeenth Century Englishwomen*, London: Routledge, 1999.

GREAVES, Richard L. and ZALLER, Robert, *Biographical Dictionary of British Radicals in the Seventeenth Century*, Brighton: Harvester, 1984.

GWYNN, Douglas, *The Covenant Crucified*, Pennsylvania: Pendle Hill, 199.

GWYNN, Douglas, *Seekers Found, Atonement in Early Quaker Experience*, Pennsylvania: Pendle Hill, 2000.

HANNAY, Margaret, *Silent But For The Word: Tudor Women As Patrons, Translators*, Kent (Ohio): Kent State University Press, 1985.

HAZELTON, Meiling, 'Mony Choaks, The Quaker Critique of the Seventeenth-Century Public Sphere,' *Modern Philology*, 98, (2), Nov. 2000, pp.251-271.

HILL, Christopher, *The English Bible and the Seventeenth Century Revolution*, London: Allen Lane, 1993.

HILL, Christopher, *The World Turned Upside Down*, York: Viking, 1972.

HINDS, Hilary, *Strength in Weakness Manifest: Women's writings from the Radical Sects of the Seventeenth Century*, Thesis (Ph.D.), Birmingham: University of Birmingham, Dept of English, 1987.

HINDS, Hilary, *God's Englishwomen*, Manchester: Manchester University Press, 1996.

HOBBY, Elaine, *Virtue of Necessity: English Women's Writing 1646-1688*, London: Virago Press, 1988.

HUBER, Elaine C., 'A Woman Must Not Speak: Quaker Women in the English Left Wing,' Reuther, Rosemary Radford and McLaughlin, Eleanor (eds), *Women of Spirit : Female Leadership in the Jewish and Christian Traditions*, New York: Simon and Schuster, 1979.

HUFTON, Olwen, *The Prospect Before Her: A History of Women in Western Europe,* 1, 1500-1800, London: Harper Collins,1995.

INGLE, H. Larry, *First Among Friends: George Fox and the Creation of Quakerism,* Oxford: Oxford University Press, 1985.

JARDINE, Lisa and GRAFTON, Anthony, *From Humanism To The Humanities: Education and the Liberal Arts in Fifteenth and Sixteenth Century Europe,* London: Duckworth, 1986.

JONES, Rufus M., *Spiritual Reformers in the Sixteenth and Seventeenth Centuries,* Boston: Beacon Hill, 1959.

KONKOLA, Kari, 'People of the Book: The Production of Theological Texts in Early Modern England, *The Proceedings of the Bibliographical Society of America,* 94 (1) 2000, pp.5-33, London, 1994.

KUNZE, Bonnelyn Young, *Margaret Fell and the Rise of Quakerism,* London: MacMillan, 1994.

LEWALSKI, Barbara Kiefer, *Writing Women in Jacobean England,* Cambridge: Cambridge University Press, 1993.

LLOYD, Arnold, *Quaker Social History,* London: Longman, 1950.

LUDLOW, Dorothy P., 'Shaking Patriarchy's Foundations: Sectarian Women in England, 1641-1700,' Greaves, Richard L. (ed), *Triumph Over Silence: Women in Protestant History,* London: Greenwood Press: 1985.

LUXON, Thomas, H., 'Not I but Christ: Allegory and the Puritan Self,' *English Literary History,* 60, (4), 1993, pp.899-937.

LYNCH, Kathleen, 'Her Name Agnes: The Verification of Agnes Beaumont's Narrative Ventures,' *English Literary History,* 67, 2000, pp.71-98.

MACK, Phyllis, *Visionary Women,* California: University of California Press, 1992.

MCGREGOR, J.F. and REAY, B., *Radical Religion in the English Revolution,* Oxford: Clarendon Press.

MASSEY, Vera: *James Nayler: the Clouded Quaker Star,* Sessions Book Trust in association with Friends United Press, Richmond, Indiana, 1999.

MENDELSON, Sara Heller, *The Mental World of Stuart Women, Three Studies,* Cambridge, Massachusetts: Harvard University Press, 1987.

METZGER, M. Bruce and COOGAN, Michael D., *The Oxford Companion to the Bible,* Oxford: Oxford University Press, 1993.

MOORE, Rosemary, *The Light in their Consciences, Early Quakers in Britain, 1646-1666,* Pennsylvania: Pendle Hill, 2000.

NICKALLS, John, L., (ed.) *The Journal of George Fox,* London: Religious Society of Friends, 1975.

NIMMO, Dorothy, *James Nayler a Testimony:* Narrative Poem, Sessions Book Trust, 1993.

NOBLE, Vernon, *The Man in Leather Breeches, The Life and Times of George Fox,* London: Elek, 1953.

OTTEN, Charlotte F., (ed.) *English Women's Voices, 1540-1700,* Miami: Florida International University Press, 1992.

PENNINGTON, Norman, (ed.) *Journal of George Fox,* Cambridge: Cambridge University Press, 1911.

PRIOR, Mary, *Women in English Society, 1500-1800,* London: Routledge, 1985.

QUAKER STUDIES, 'Rebellious Quaker Women (1650-1660)', by Catie Gill, pp.25-27 & 30.

REAY, Barry, *The Quakers and the English Revolution,* London: Temple Smith, 1985.

REUTHER, Rosemary Radford, 'Quaker Women Prophets in England and Wales,' *Studies in Women and Religion,* 41, 2000, pp.

REUTHER, Rosemary Radford, 'Prophets and Humanists: Types of Religious Feminism in Stuart England,' *Journal of Religion,* 70, 1990, pp.1-18.

ROSS, Isabel, *Margaret Fell: Mother of Quakerism,* Sessions, reprinted 1996.

SMART, Ninian, *The World's Religions,* Cambridge: Cambridge University Press, 1997.

SMITH, Hilda and CARDINALE, Susan, *Literature of the Seventeenth Century: An Annotated Bibliography based on Wing's Short Title Catalogue,* New York: Greenwood Press, 1990.

SMITH, Nigel, *Perfection Proclaimed, Language and Literature in English Radical Religion, 1640-1660,* Oxford: Clarendon Press, 1989.

SMITH, Nigel, *Literature and Revolution in England, 1640-1660,* New Haven and London: Yale University Press, 1999.

SPENCER, Carol, 'James Nayler: Antinomian or Perfectionist?' *Quaker Studies,* 6 (1), 2001, pp.106-117.

TAYLOR, Ernest E., *The Valiant Sixty,* Sessions, reprinted 1988.

TRAVITSKY, Betty, (ed.) *The Paradise Of Women: Writings By English Women of the Renaissance,* New York: Columbia University Press, 1989.

TREVETT, Christine, *Women and Quakerism in the Seventeenth Century,* York: Sessions Book Trust, 1991.

TREVETT, Christine, 'The Women around James Nayler, Quaker: A Matter of Emphasis,' *Religion*, 20, 1990, pp.249-273.

WATTS, Michael R., *The Dissenters: From the Reformation to the French Revolution*, Oxford: Clarendon Press, 1978.

WHITE, Micheline, 'Renaissance Englishwomen and Religious Translations: The Case of Anne Lock's Of the Marks of the Children of God', *English Literary Renaissance*, 29 (3) 1999, pp.375-400.

WILLIAMS, Ethyn Morgan, 'Women Preachers in the Civil War,' *Journal of Modern History*, 1, (4), 1929. pp.561-569.

WISEMAN, S., 'Margaret Cavendish among the Prophets: performance ideologies and gender in an after the English Civil War,' *Women's Writing*, 6, (1) 1999, pp.99-111.

WRIGHT, Luella, *The Literary Life of Early Friends, 1650-1725*, New York: Columbia University Press, 1932.